**CCCC STUDIES IN WRITING & RH**

*Edited by Joseph Harris, Duke Unive*

The aim of the CCCC Studies in Writing & Rhetoric Series is to influence how we think about language in action and especially how writing gets taught at the college level. The methods of studies vary from the critical to historical to linguistic to ethnographic, and their authors draw on work in various fields that inform composition—including rhetoric, communication, education, discourse analysis, psychology, cultural studies, and literature. Their focuses are similarly diverse—ranging from individual writers and teachers, to work on classrooms and communities and curricula, to analyses of the social, political, and material contexts of writing and its teaching.

SWR was one of the first scholarly book series to focus on the teaching of writing. It was established in 1980 by the Conference on College Composition and Communication (CCCC) in order to promote research in the emerging field of writing studies. As our field has grown, the research sponsored by SWR has continued to articulate the commitment of CCCC to supporting the work of writing teachers as reflective practitioners and intellectuals.

We are eager to identify influential work in writing and rhetoric as it emerges. We thus ask authors to send us project proposals that clearly situate their work in the field and show how they aim to redirect our ongoing conversations about writing and its teaching. Proposals should include an overview of the project, a brief annotated table of contents, and a sample chapter. They should not exceed 10,000 words.

To submit a proposal, please register as an author at www.editorial manager.com/nctebp. Once registered, follow the steps to submit a proposal (be sure to choose SWR Book Proposal from the drop-down list of article submission types).

# AGENCY IN THE AGE OF PEER PRODUCTION

## Quentin D. Vieregge
*University of Wisconsin–Barron County*

## Kyle D. Stedman
*Rockford College*

## Taylor Joy Mitchell
*University of South Florida*

## Joseph M. Moxley
*University of South Florida*

Conference on College Composition and Communication

National Council of Teachers of English

Staff Editor: Bonny Graham
Interior Design: Mary Rohrer
Cover Design: Mary Rohrer and Lynn Weckhorst

NCTE Stock Number: 00899

It is the policy of NCTE in its journals and other publications to provide a forum for the open discussion of ideas concerning the content and the teaching of English and the language arts. Publicity accorded to any particular point of view does not imply endorsement by the Executive Committee, the Board of Directors, or the membership at large, except in announcements of policy, where such endorsement is clearly specified.

Every effort has been made to provide current URLs and email addresses, but because of the rapidly changing nature of the Web, some sites and addresses may no longer be accessible.

Publication partially funded by a subvention grant from the Conference on College Composition and Communication of the National Council of Teachers of English.

**Library of Congress Cataloging-in-Publication Data**
Vieregge, Quentin D., 1979-
  Agency in the age of peer production / Quentin D. Vieregge . . . [et al.].
    p. cm. — (CCCC Studies in Writing & Rhetoric)
  Includes bibliographical references and index.
  ISBN 978-0-8141-0089-9 (pbk : alk. paper)
1. English language—Rhetoric—Study and teaching (Higher)—United States.
2. English language—Rhetoric—Study and teaching (Higher)—Technological innovations. 3. Report writing—Study and teaching (Higher)—United States.
4. Internet in education. I. National Council of Teachers of English. II. Conference on College Composition and Communication (U.S.) III. Title.
  PE1405.U6V44 2012
  808'.042071173—dc23
                                                              2012008163

# CONTENTS

## ACKNOWLEDGMENTS

AS RESEARCHERS WRITING ABOUT THE community we are embedded in—even while that community changes somewhat from year to year—we are incredibly grateful to our colleagues and critics.

Our thanks go to the graduate students, adjuncts, staff, and faculty who have helped build our composition program. Megan McIntyre, Jessica McKee, Daniel Richards, Susan Taylor, Erin Trauth, and Jennifer Yirinec have played key leadership roles, changing the course of the program. We thank all of the FYC faculty and mentors, especially the first-year composition teachers we interviewed. We thank Drs. Dianne Donnelly, Kim Murray, and Michael Shuman for their service as associate directors of the writing program. Dr. Terry Beavers deserves special recognition for his tireless, creative efforts at building the infrastructure for our program's websites and assessment tools.

We also thank Deedra Hickman for her wizardry with data visualization tools, Katelin Kaiser for her past four years of work as Professor Moxley's undergraduate research assistant, and Nancy Serrano for her steady, timely, and thorough work as our budget director.

We extend our gratitude to Kate Pantelides, Marc Santos, and Meredith Zoetewey for reading and rereading our manuscript and offering valuable feedback.

And many administrative figures made this work a possibility: Hunt Hawkins, Janet Moore, Steve RiCharde, and Diane Williams. A special thanks goes to the General Education Council, particularly Gladis Kersaint and Karla Davis-Salazar, for its continued funding of our mentoring program. Finally, we thank the FYC Policy Committee for its insights and advisory role.

**AGENCY IN THE AGE OF PEER PRODUCTION**

# Introduction

WE BEGIN WITH AN EARTHQUAKE—an investigation of how peer production has shaken communication, education, and agency. Peer-production tools are shifting the nature of communication and collaboration in the twenty-first century, and this change is already transforming the ways students, teachers, and writing program administrators talk to or write with one another. Communication between teachers and students can occur through numerous channels now: in the office or online, synchronously or asynchronously. Administrators and students can contact each other much more easily, and teachers can share ideas and lesson plans individually or in groups. One effect of all these changes is that classrooms no longer need be thought of as discrete spheres, separated by four walls and a closed door from the rest of a writing program or department as soon as the first day of class begins. In other words, peer-production tools provide, at the very least, the promise—we recognize they also represent several possible pitfalls—of increased collaboration.

This book was born out of the hope that we could explore the implications of some of those promises and pitfalls through an introspective qualitative study. The four of us write as administrators and qualitative researchers. Our study focuses on a five-year effort to understand how peer-production tools—and, more important, the ideas and values behind peer production—influence the agency of teachers.

In this "age of peer production," a phrase coined by Chris Anderson, words, images, videos, and sounds can be easily shared, debated, and developed over today's networked computers. Instead of feeling alone, isolated behind closed classroom doors, focused on books printed five, ten, even twenty years ago, today's educators can collaborate on documents, pedagogies, and assessments in unprecedented ways with peer-production technologies, asserting a teacherly agency by banding together to create ideas and practices that are better than the sum of what any teacher could have developed alone. The age of peer production can mean technological innovations such as wikis, blogs, and video-sharing and social networking sites; but we believe it also needs to include offline efforts such as mentoring programs, orientation meetings, brown-bag luncheons, and the general ethos of a sharing community. If peer production is to assume its own "age," then it must be more about values than about tools, which are replaceable and easily outdated.

Of course, things are never as utopian as we imagine they could be. This study tells the stories—both successes and failures—we experienced when we experimented with peer-production tools to fundamentally change the nature of composition teachers' agency at a large research university. We found that in many instances these technologies did positively affect the experiences of our teachers and students, as well as our program's standing in our university, but we also found that these tech-driven innovations had to be balanced by serious investment in developing face-to-face community. By investigating the changing nature of agency and communication through the lens of our experiences, we hope to alert other writing program administrators, university leaders, and classroom instructors to the possibilities and obstacles awaiting them as new technologies and attitudes shift traditional power relations.

We hope readers come away from our study with a set of practical guidelines and a more general theoretical understanding of how peer production works. We focus on both the practical and the philosophical because both forms of knowledge have their place depending on who is reading this book, when, and for what purposes. For the purposes of this introduction, we might think of this as everyday "know-how" knowledge versus more theoretical "know-why" knowledge. Our interview chapters are aimed at the particular and idiosyncratic experiences of our program's administrators and instructors. Throughout these chapters, and especially at the end of each one, we reference the everyday, evolving, know-how knowledge. We tried some things; sometimes they failed, so we tried again and they worked. Our program's teachers collaborated in inspiring ways, and so we asked, "How?" This knowledge is intuitive and incremental. To the extent that our readers share similar programs or interpersonal dynamics with teachers and students, they may gain from the know-how. In Chapters 1 and 5, we theorize about the know-why. Rather than create a single monologic concept of agency, we offer several characteristics and patterns that represent a theory of agency in the age of peer production within the context of university writing programs. The final chapter also generalizes some of the know-how lessons.

Part of what catalyzes the story of our program is the push and pull between teachers and administrators. The subtext of our book is the friction that exists—and the sparks that sometimes fly— when the need for individual agency among instructors meets the necessity for a shared curriculum. The book and the program on which it is based are in part an experiment about whether these two forces can be compatible and even mutually reinforcing in the age of peer production. Is it possible for both individual and communal agency to coexist, and if so, what kind of underlife, or unofficial connections and networking, might emerge from that relationship? Perhaps many instructors in large first-year composition (FYC) programs—specifically those at research universities where graduate students and adjunct instructors teach most sections— share these concerns. These instructors may face a set of seemingly impossible tasks: they must show themselves to be creative teachers within the confines of department syllabi; they must support university and assessment policies while trying not to "teach to the test"; they must lean on the newest and best composition pedagogy and theory without sacrificing their own particular pedagogical goals; and they must adapt to ever-changing program requirements without losing the work they've put into each of their classes. Since many of these instructors have training outside the field of rhetoric and composition, they must work in two scholastic worlds, bringing to the classroom their knowledge in literature, creative writing, or communication while at the same time learning the composition pedagogy they might not be familiar with. But they believe in the mission of their university. They want to play along without being *pushed* along. They want to assert their own agency without completely delegitimizing the agency of their programs, departments, and colleges.

In smaller two-year or four-year schools there exists, if in different ways, the same tension between the agency of the teacher and the need for overarching programmatic goals. In such schools, the majority of the instructors may have decades of experience and be well versed in many different writing pedagogies. Unlike in large state universities, there may be little or no need for training inexperienced graduate teaching associates, for scaffolding instructor training with standardized syllabi, or for as much top-down administrative control. But a community of experienced faculty still needs to develop a shared curriculum. The benefits of collective intelligence remain. Such departments may still feel the need to make certain the first-year composition experience feels like a coherent whole either across sections or from the first semester to the second semester. They may value a collaborative pedagogical atmosphere in which teachers share lesson plans, teaching methods, strengths, and struggles. Each course may share a similar set of objectives or learning goals between its individual sections, even if the faculty approaches those objectives in creative ways. These demands would require teachers to balance individuality with collaboration, the expression of their unique talents with the need for a shared curriculum. Furthermore, these departments and their instructors may benefit from the "wisdom of the crowds" and collective intelligence, which are afforded by peer-production tools (Surowiecki).

Chapter 1 introduces the broad societal importance of these peer-production technologies, considering how the seismic shifts in how people collaborate intersect with questions of agency—questions of how power relations are affected when everyone has the theoretical and computing power to speak in a conversation. We introduce here our dual vision of agency, a dialectical relationship between individual and communal power. Chapter 2 then moves from these broad discussions into the specific contexts of our university and our FYC program, including our budgetary constraints, our efforts at building a teaching community, and our program technologies. This chapter also describes the methods used to collect the stories told in Chapters 3 through 5, which rely on teacher interviews and archival data collected at our university.

Chapters 3 through 5 focus on our primary research, including surveys, listserv archives, data from our online rubric, usage statistics from our program's website, and the interviews we conducted with our instructors over the course of a year. Chapter 3, the first of our interview-centered chapters, describes our efforts to create a culture of assessment based on our online rubric tool. We contrast our own expectations and objectives when we started the rubric with the initial and subsequent responses by graduate students and adjunct instructors as they began to grade with it. In Chapter 4, we study how our instructors formed self-guided groups while learning how to teach in our technology-heavy program. We asked them to identify themselves in terms of their level of technological and curricular innovation and how their self-identification related to the organic groups they formed in shared offices and in the halls. These groups are the centrifugal forces that push outward, away from administrative control. In Chapter 5, we contrast these groups with the centripetal forces exerted through our mentoring program. The mentoring program attempts to blend face-to-face and online collaboration to guide incoming graduate students new to our program and to teaching. Chapter 6 sums up our vision of this ecology's elements along with a series of specific suggestions for how other composition programs and networked organizations can learn from our successes and shortcomings. Following a year of qualitative research, which has involved in-depth interviews with twenty-six instructors, survey results from thirteen more, and a review of our archived emails and surveys since 2004, we have found that face-to-face interactions and our mentoring program are a crucial part of our online efforts to encourage agency, community, and a shared curriculum.

It was critical for us to tell these stories from the dual perspective of our teachers and ourselves as staff of the FYC program; the big-picture perspective of administrators is necessarily different from the viewpoint of those who actually experience the day-to-day difficulties of following (and subverting) orders from above. We report our examples multivocally by quoting our teachers within our own big-picture explanations. In this sense, a book cowritten by four individuals, each with full drafting and editing abilities on each chapter, is beneficial, as it reflects the emphasis on multiple perspectives that is at the heart of the book—and, indeed, at the heart of our vision of how power can be shared and enhanced by collective action. The voice of our writing program administrator, Joe, is joined by those of three advanced graduate students, Quentin, Kyle, and Taylor, all of whom taught extensively in our FYC program as well as labored to develop its curriculum, Web resources, and community in different ways over multiple years.

But let us examine these tectonic shifts in agency and peer production in more detail.

# 1

## Peer Production and Tectonic Shifts in Agency

*How do commons-based peer-production tools alter how teachers and writing program administrators find agency—that is, broadly speaking, the ability to affect change? How might peer-production tools be used in educational settings, particularly writing programs, to enhance teaching and learning, avoid "courseocentrism," and foster both communal and individual agency?*

OVER A DECADE INTO THE twenty-first century, literacy practices are changing seismically. Thanks to new writing spaces, we are redefining what it means to read, research, write, and share texts. These texts take the form of new genres that emerge in response to new media, such as hypertextual poems, cell phone novels, and collaboratively written essays or song lyrics composed online with strangers. Everyone now has an opportunity to be a Thomas Paine or Johannes Gutenberg, to espouse an individualized common sense through a blog or website. Aphorists pen new witticisms on Facebook for friends and email is seen by first-year students as an "old" way to write. The landscape of literacy has shifted underneath our feet, and we are only just beginning the job of the cartographer, redrawing—for the first time in hundreds of years—the maps of how classrooms will dramatically change. This literacy transformation inevitably impacts who can effect change, who can have agency, and how, and even where, literacy instruction should take place.

Social networking and peer-production tools are overlapping but distinct phenomena that create new communities online and provide opportunities for communities to exist offline. Social networking sites typically connect friends, colleagues, and those who share common interests by helping to form groups that otherwise might never coalesce; just as often, these sites maintain relationships that might grow cold or distant without an online dimension supporting them. Social networks encourage personal expression and the viral spread of ideas through sharing a hashtag or following a colleague on Twitter, joining a cause on Facebook or subscribing to a channel on YouTube. But social networks are also like digital Rolodexes: they provide easy access to a lifetime's worth of acquaintances who, simply because of their close digital proximity, may later become one's future collaborators. The most obvious examples of social networking sites—Facebook, Twitter, and LinkedIn—appear to some to be associated with a youth-centered American culture, but these sites are quickly burning cultural borders and age boundaries. For instance, Facebook reports its "fastest growing demographic is those 35 years old and older" ("Statistics"). The website exceeds an online population of 750 million, and one out of every two of those users logs in daily. With photos, notes, news stories, and links counted in the billions, and millions of videos, Facebook is a repository of information. The site can be read in scores of languages, and surprisingly, most of Facebook's users live beyond the boundaries of North America. And these numbers change rapidly; since this chapter was first drafted and later edited, Facebook's statistics page announced an increase of 300 million users in a single academic year. When you read this, the numbers will surely have blossomed again.

At the same time, the rise of peer-production tools has mirrored the growth of social networking; individuals increasingly turn to robust computer networks for friendship, collaboration, and meaning making. Peer-production technologies have attributes similar to those of social networking sites, but instead of encouraging personal expression, the viral spread of ideas, and networking, peer-production communities are more like twenty-first-century barn building (Benkler and Nissenbaum 395). These tools allow for massive acts of collaborative creation by asking for just a little effort from each contributor. As espoused by both scholarly authors (Benkler; Brown and Duguid; boyd and Ellison; Cummings and

Barton; Jenkins) and trade book authors (Li and Bernoff; Gillmor; Tapscott and Williams; Weinberger), peer-production tools democratize power, redistributing the means of production from a one-way communication model, like a CBS broadcasting tower, to an increasingly community-driven model, in which individuals contribute freely and democratically. Some well-known examples of peer production include the now ubiquitous Wikipedia, the crowd-sourced operating system Linux, and the news aggregator Slashdot, where people share and comment on technology-themed articles they've discovered (Benkler and Nissenbaum 395–98). These are all sites where large groups share resources or ideas for a central purpose (or many networked mini-purposes), giving individuals the ability to participate in large-scale action. As Chris Anderson noted in 2006, we've landed in the age of peer production.

Peer-production technologies are more powerful than they might at first seem: they allow users to add content, which affects the way knowledge is constructed. Popular online communities have altered how communities are established; how individuals define themselves; how knowledge is created, published, and disseminated; and how friendships are defined and constructed. Wikipedia editors write, link, and comment on texts knowing that they can expect a significant readership (including, of course, Wikipedia's community editors, who track changes and occasionally undo changes) (Benkler 72). Contributors to YouTube create channels, promote the work of others by linking outside of the site, and receive commentary from viewers. Amazon and eBay users can promote or marginalize sellers by positive or negative commentary, creating winners and losers in the global marketplace through the aggregation of common wisdom (Benkler 75). SETI (the Search for Extraterrestrial Intelligence) is a project that aggregates the processing power of millions of personal computers to analyze "data sets collected from large radio telescope observations" (Benkler and Nissenbaum 396). These peer-production communities have reshuffled power relations, enabling individuals to influence the shape and direction of modern life, world markets, elections, and public opinion about seminal matters such as global warming and energy policies.

Perhaps the most intriguing idea to emerge from the evolution of social media and peer production is the possibility of collective intelligence, the notion that crowds of people working collaboratively by means of an online tool such as Wikipedia can create ideas that are unique and smarter than the ideas of individuals. James Surowiecki, George Siemens, Henry Jenkins, and Howard Rheingold have all theorized that peer-production tools empower users to create a new "emergent" knowledge that individuals working alone could not develop. Peer-production technologies change the ways we exchange ideas, organize ourselves, and create knowledge (Weinberger; Shirky; Jenkins); encourage democratic decision making (Benkler; Shirky; Rheingold); transform how people write and think about themselves (Lanier); and encourage ethical behavior (Benkler and Nissenbaum). It's only natural, then, that they also change how we organize our institutions of higher learning (Taylor).

## PEER PRODUCTION IN FIRST-YEAR COMPOSITION

As writing program administrators (WPAs) at a large state university (hereafter called Research University [RU]) responsible for teaching two courses of first-year composition (ENC 1101 and ENC 1102), we were especially curious to learn how to adapt our curriculum to respond to new literacies, collaborative tools, and modes of knowledge making. Equally challenging, we wondered how we could employ peer-production tools to open classrooms to informed collaboration between instructors. And beyond using peer production's online innovations for classroom collaboration, how could the offline, face-to-face efforts of peer production be used to create a general ethos of sharing needed for twenty-first-century instruction? We were curious about the ways these tools could reshape the role of WPAs and teachers.

Hence, in fall 2004, we began using a variety of peer-production tools to develop a shared pedagogy that relied on the contributions from our teachers and students. Rather than follow the traditional top-down hierarchical structure of a writing program, in which tenured faculty define a curriculum or import one from publishers or theorists, we hoped to develop a datagogical model: a collaborative model for pedagogical innovation that enables everyone—tenured and adjunct faculty, graduate students, and even undergraduates—to engage in an ongoing effort to refine and improve our curriculum, based on dialogue, argument, and evidence (Moxley, "Datagogies"). We hoped that these peer-production technologies would allow us a fresh way to increase the opportunity for democratic decision making. For instance, composition programs have often valued voice and a socially constructivist pedagogy; they have emphasized decentralizing power, democratizing knowledge, and creating connections between various disciplines (Shor and Freire; Gunner, "Collaborative"). Our use of wikis in the writing program, for instance, was an example of collective groups of individuals coming together in a way that diminishes (though does not eliminate) the influence of traditionally silencing power structures. Transparency comes in the form of the history pages on wikis that carefully document every change made by each user and allow users/editors to revert to older versions of texts. Discussion boards also maintain transparency, by invoking dialogue and calling for users to justify their content changes inside the digital public sphere. Moreover, by making programmatic decisions contingent on rational discourse, we decentralized power so that decisions could then be made based on dialogue and argumentation rather than authority. In this sense, our digital public sphere harkens back to Jürgen Habermas and his discussion of the transformation of the public sphere. One of his arguments is that the Enlightenment brought about a bourgeois public sphere, "in which the private people, come together to form a public, readied themselves to compel public authority to legitimate itself before public opinion" (25–26). This public contested the decision-making authority of the "prince" and of the "ruling estates," pressing for reasoned debate as the foundation for political power. Thus, the sphere of public authority and that of the private realm became intertwined. We viewed our peer-production technologies as furthering a Habermasian model of public discourse by decentralizing power and encouraging debate.

Initially, we hoped our primary writing portal would represent an online market street, with each merchant bringing his or her own specialties: worthwhile activities to engage recalcitrant students, worksheets that help teach thesis statements, ideas for introducing the concepts of style and voice, annotated lists of movies for a film ethics project, links to websites that easily explain rhetorical terminology, or new YouTube videos that spark teachable moments. Teachers would exchange ideas in this city square, watch videos of best practices by other instructors, and cowrite the curriculum online, guided by common shared outcomes, course policies, mission statements, and governance documents. This city square would not adopt a laissez-faire attitude: administrative voices would frame online academic conversations around institutional concerns unfamiliar to instructors. For instance, an instructor's idea to introduce a memoir or social action project would be discussed in terms of the writing program's relationship to RU's general educational curriculum. Likewise, complaints regarding resources would be reframed as administrative requests for technology funding. Certainly not everyone would be an equal contributor—some would shop, others would sell—but our digital space would have a cultural currency. Whenever instructors had or needed an idea, they would go to our program's website. Rather than a marketplace tied to gold, our marketplace's ethos would be that of a "gift culture," and the currency would be academic pride. Of course, our metaphor of the marketplace implies money as the animating force behind it, and this obviously contradicts the objective to create a "gift culture" within the program. But this seeming contradiction is exactly the point: we were hoping peer-production tools would be a game changer, something that would transform the well-worn business motto "What gets rewarded, gets done" to a variation on President Kennedy's famous call to action, "Ask not what your colleagues can do for you but what you can do for your colleagues."

We pursued these hopes with a variety of peer-production tools, including an extensive public website, a password-protected intranet accessible solely by our teachers, a listserv, and a gated online assessment tool.[1] We also supplemented these tools with nontechnical, community-building events, including an extensive mentoring program, a two-week intensive orientation program, instructional videos, podcasts, newsletters, and various other face-to-face community-building and training activities, including softball games, brown-bag lunch presentations, kayaking and rappelling adventures, and guest speakers.

Between 2004 and 2009, however, we increasingly realized that engaging writing program faculty in a shared effort to develop a sound pedagogy was much more complicated than first presumed. Our marketplace of ideas had fluctuated between vibrant and anemic depending on the time of year, our instructor population, the usability of our websites, campus politics, and program funding. We could identify some successes and some disappointments. When we took an honest look at who participated, it seemed that a core group of graduate students and adjuncts was collaborating with one another to develop our shared pedagogy, revise our curriculum with a focus on outcomes, produce textbooks, develop new major writing projects, edit old projects, rewrite program policies, offer training sessions for other instructors, and contribute to the development of our online rubric tool. During these first six years, this core group of instructors assumed unprecedented leadership roles in the writing program. Happily, some of these leaders presented their contributions at professional conferences, in published papers, and during job searches.

Yet from ongoing talks with instructors, we were also made aware of significant failures—failures that at times made our hopes of creating a gift culture seem too Pollyannaish, failures that at times made us want to return to more traditional hierarchical models. Why? Even after six years of daily effort, we found that the majority of instructors resisted our invitations to participate in our community, either online or face to face. From informal conversations with instructors, we found some had mistaken our emphasis on shared outcomes as an effort to homogenize instruction—to control them rather than engage them in sustained dialogue about best practices.

Even with a variety of opportunities for collaboration, program critique, and development, some faculty still resisted engaging with our writing program.

Without much effort, we could point to several possible reasons we could not engage the majority of instructors in our collaborative efforts. We knew, for example, that our emphasis on collaboration was a dramatic shift from the traditional view of the teacher in the closed classroom. Indeed, the degree to which a teacher has privacy in the classroom is often seen as a sign of academic freedom. Gerald Graff reflects on this tendency—one that he admits he shares—and comes to the conclusion that "we do not appreciate the educational damage that results from teaching in self-isolated classrooms" ("Why" 157). He calls this ethos *courseocentrism*, "a kind of tunnel vision in which we become so used to the confines of our own course that we are oblivious to the fact that our students are taking other courses whose instructors at any moment may be undercutting our most cherished beliefs" (157). What we viewed as freedom, the opportunity to collaborate on programmatic changes, was viewed by some instructors as an encroachment on their private classroom space.

We also understood basic impediments to their engagement. Many instructors did not use our peer-production tools because they lacked the necessary training—and, admittedly, some of the tools we had chosen were not the easiest to use. Also, we were well aware of the long history of teachers' resistance to standardization. And we understood that the transitory nature of our community likely impinged on its overall effectiveness: most of our teachers graduate from the program or begin to teach higher-level courses.

Furthermore, we were aware that our experiences were similar to the experiences of other communities that have used social software; even though the Wikipedia community might seem at first glance to have engaged hundreds of thousands of users in authoring the online encyclopedia, the reality is that most pages are predominantly written by a small number of dedicated users—perhaps only 20 percent—while another 80 percent made minimal, if collectively significant, changes, a distribution of engagement so widespread across human phenomena (e.g., economics, writing, collaboration) that it is sometimes called the "80–20 rule," or Pareto's principle (Shirky 126). The 80–20 rule has been a lens helping us understand human relations "since Vilfredo Pareto, an Italian economist working in the early 1900s, found a power law distribution of wealth" (Shirky 126). More recently, collaboration theorists have applied it to social software and any large organizational structure. For example, even though the ongoing development of various Linux platforms has involved thousands of users worldwide, only a "handful" of programmers produce the actual "core" program (Shirky 250–51). Consequently, we struggle to accurately reconcile the dynamics of the 80–20 rule with our program, and we wonder what factors motivate participation in our effort to develop a shared pedagogy. Intriguingly, the rule follows a *power-law distribution*, a term describing this kind of mathematical relationship and one that we find coincidentally appropriate, given our interest in how power is distributed across a composition program.

While we found the 80–20 rule to be reassuring, and while we recognized that our culture's emphasis on individual achievement and theoretical scholarship could partially explain teachers' reluctance to join our collaborative efforts, we wondered if many of the benefits of peer-production tools pertained primarily to nonmarket, nonhierarchical contexts as opposed to our academic context. After all, peer-production miracles like Wikipedia or Newsvine are global phenomena, "large-and medium-scale collaborations among individuals, organized without markets or managerial hierarchies" (Benkler and Nissenbaum 400). The power of peer-production tools employed by these communities does not necessarily reflect workplace relationships or learning communities within higher education, which are propelled as much (if not more) by pay, academic recognition, hierarchical control, and the pressure to publish.

Ultimately, then, we began this research because we wanted to do more than hide behind the feel-good implications of the 80–20 rule. If anyone ever asked us whether our effort was as successful as Wikipedia or other socially driven sites, we didn't want to claim, "Oh yeah, we've got at least 10 to 20 percent of our teachers involved in our shared effort to develop our curriculum, assessment, and program polices." Plus, we wanted to see how well peer production could be employed in our workplace context, a large state university. When Yochai Benkler and Martha Nissenbaum wrote about the prevalence of virtue in peer-production sites, they focused on nonworkplace environments. These environments do not include several variables essential to a workplace setting, especially ones that can affect a group's cohesion and motivation. Employees—as opposed to Internet volunteers—are especially concerned with financial compensation, career ambition, and compulsory obligations, and so we were intrigued to see how peer-production tools could be used to create a gift culture in this type of setting. After all, the ability to give a gift, whether in person or in a digital network environment, is in one sense the ability to act on one's own, free from outside restraints. But in a university setting, faculty are always hampered by multiple, outside restraints, to both their benefit and their detriment. Therefore, how can individuals assert their own agency even as they are surrounded by the needs of wider communities?

### INDIVIDUAL AND COMMUNAL AGENCY

When evaluating our research goals, we determined that we wanted to analyze agency on at least two levels, the individual and the communal (see Figure 1.1). We hoped to learn more about the complex relationship between individual and communal agency that is at the heart of our program, because we realized our instructors daily meet multiple responsibilities to their students, the administration, and their own academic studies. At times some of these responsibilities—meeting common course objectives, teaching a shared curriculum, and collaborating during orientation—appear to work in contravention to an instructor's desire to individually instruct his or her students with his or her own talents. In contrast, we also realized that our shared curriculum increased the credibility of the composition program by validating student grades and by showing that what happens within each classroom matches RU's learning outcomes.

**Figure 1.1. The elements of agency**

Several rhetoric scholars have observed that the term *agency* implies two seemingly contradictory ideas: that writers have both free will independent of outside constraints and that their voices are determined by the institutions to which they belong. Scholars like John Trimbur argue that agency operates at personal and communal levels but see this seeming contradiction as an opportunity for individuals to effect change. James E. Porter, Patricia Sullivan, Stuart Blythe, Jeffrey T. Grabill, and Libby Miles argue that institutions are composed of humans who can rewrite the structures of the organizations to which they belong. They argue, "[T]hough institutions are certainly powerful, they are not monoliths; they are rhetorically constructed human designs (whose power is reinforced by buildings, laws, traditions, and knowledge-making practices) and so are changeable" (Porter et al. 611). Blythe, in particular, has argued in subsequent scholarship that "the paradox of agency" is that "[w]e gain it not by being an autonomous individual, but by being part of something larger, by being a part of systems that constrain and enable simultaneously" (173). Whether in the realm of business, journalism, or law, we could point to countless examples of how people find their voices individually and effect change by becoming a part of something larger—a force that works similarly in educational contexts (Blythe). For instructors to effect change and affect their worlds, they need to have both personal autonomy and communal identity.

One possible example of this dual vision of agency might be a blog carnival—a collaborative effort by different bloggers to approach a single topic on their own blogs and from their own points of view, with all responses collated into a single repository. For example, in July 2008, compositionist Derek Mueller wrote a blog post asking for submissions to a carnival discussing a recent article in *College Composition and Communication* (Mueller). Several scholars posted opinions on the article on their own blogs, each of which was linked from the carnival call page. Certainly, all of the participating authors enjoyed the discursive agency implied in the act of blogging: unrestrained by institutional demands, they were free to insert themselves into the story of the article and stake a claim in the scholarly conversation. However, the communal nature of the blog carnival added a new level of agency to the collection of blog posts. After all, a single academic blogger, even with a comparatively sizable readership, would be unable to have the impact afforded by the collective action of the carnival; the splash of a single post is necessarily smaller than the belly flop of a group of organized, intelligent, individualized-yet-connected posts all dropping into the ether of online space at the same time. Agency, in this case, is held both by individuals and by the group, depending on the observer's point of view and focus. And ideally, teaching communities can work the same way, with the efforts of single teachers thriving both on their own and in the context of a connected, empowered group.

Hence, in 2009 to 2010, we employed archival, case study, and ethnographic methods to investigate what motivates composition faculty at our university to join, and feel agency within, our online and face-to-face teaching community. As a result, this research employs case study and ethnographic methods to investigate how social media and peer-production tools have impacted the agency of instructors, smaller subgroups within our larger community, and WPAs. We wanted to know whether we could leverage peer-production tools to develop a shared curriculum that preserves our academic freedom. If a writing program can aggregate the ideas, generosity, and contributions of each faculty member—regardless of experience—then there is an enormous potential to create a curriculum that validates the perspectives of many different instructors. Furthermore, using peer-production tools could help writing programs shape their own futures rather than having them defined by university administrators or state or federal politicians.

## NOTE

1. This list excludes tools and sites that we have abandoned, such as a public wiki site, a public blog site, and a wiki site just for teachers.

## 2

Contexts and Research Questions

*What is life like for students, teachers, and writing program administrators at Research University? How does the collaborative Internet site for our FYC program guide the work of administrators, teachers, and students?*

IN THIS RESEARCH STUDY, we describe our community as a constant, yet our community evolves even as we try to define it. After all, our community is dynamic, led by new teachers and received by new students each year. Even more confounding, the technologies we employ vary each year—nay, each semester. While we may be unable to compose a static image of our community and its tools, we conducted the bulk of this research study over the 2009–10 academic year. We generally looked back over the recent years to gather necessary archival data to help answer our research questions. In this chapter, we address contextual factors such as our budget and the relative autonomy of our composition program. We also detail our research methods and explain the choices we made as researchers. We argue that, amidst the precarious balance for standardization and diversity, we have worked within these contexts to offer our instructors some semblance of agency. This balance directly affects our research methods and questions. Our story is one of relative institutional freedom mixed with significant budgetary roadblocks, of both programmatic excitement and miscommunication that result from a diverse student and instructor body.

### BUDGETARY CONTEXT

The lowly status of composition programs in university settings has been well documented. Since the 1960s, composition scholars have complained about their digs, insufficient funding, and lack of professional respect. Decades ago, scholars such as Sue Ellen Holbrook and Cynthia Tuell characterized composition instruction as "women's work." Holbrook's "Women's Work: The Feminizing of Composition" details four characteristics of work historically associated with women: it includes a disproportionate number of women workers, it is service oriented, it pays less than men's work, and it is devalued. Holbrook shows that when historical forces situated composition within English departments, it was relegated to a lowly status, stunted as apprentice work, and made appropriate for female instructors. Tuell's 1993 "Composition Teaching as 'Women's Work': Daughters, Handmaids, Whores, and Mothers" calls for a paradigm shift in university hierarchies and a reassessment of the value of composition instructors. Not until Mina Shaughnessy and Janet Emig initiated the discourse about invention and early process studies for basic learners did English departments begin to take notice (Wallace and Wallace). Yet even with the attention to composition of past decades, the poor working conditions of composition faculty still exist. It could be argued that working conditions have deteriorated, as universities face massive budget cuts and receive pressure nationwide to channel students toward STEM (science, technology, engineering, and math) course work.

The composition program at Research University clearly emerges from this tradition of poorly funded, poorly valued work. Not heeding Shaughnessy's warnings against basemented writing centers, our program is housed in one of the oldest buildings on campus, a building in significant disrepair. Although we are an economic engine for the College of Arts and Sciences, if not the university as a whole, we lack an independent budget and do not receive support representative of our contributions to the university as a whole. That said, we do have support from our department chair, deans, and associate provosts.

Outside of the writing program, the English department has been decimated by budget cuts and retirements. One might expect an English department at a university of our size (RU has a student body of more than 45,000) to have at least sixty tenured faculty, but due to budget cuts and hiring freezes combined with a high rate of retirees, our department employs only thirty-eight tenured faculty. There are simply not enough faculty members to teach between 130 and 200 sections of composition offered each semester—and the majority of the faculty focuses on literature, not composition. A startling 85 percent of our English department's courses are taught by graduate students or adjuncts (see Table 2.1). Our FYC instructors, during fall 2009, consisted of twenty-one first-year master of arts or master of fine arts students in creative writing, seventeen second-year MAs or MFAs, five first-year doctoral students, nine advanced PhDs, seventeen adjuncts, four visiting instructors, and zero tenure-track faculty. In the past twenty-six years, we can remember only one instance of a tenured professor teaching a composition course—and it was the director of the program, Joseph Moxley, teaching a Composition for Engineers course.

Our program instructed approximately 7,000 students in 2009–10.[1] While the majority of our students are in their first year, RU does not necessarily require their enrollment in composition during the first year, so some of our classes have upper-division students as well. Over the past five years, we have generally capped enrollment at twenty-two, although during the fall semesters in 2005 and

**Table 2.1. Makeup of FYC Instructors, Fall 2009–Spring 2010**

| Status | Number of | Sections Taught |
|---|---|---|
| 1st-Year MA/MFA | 13/8 | 21/11 |
| Advanced MA | 15 | 22 |
| Advanced MFA | 2 | 4 |
| 1st-Year PhD | 5 | 10 |
| Advanced PhD | 9 | 13 |
| Adjuncts | 30 | 74 |
| Visiting Instructors | 3 | 5 |
| Tenured Faculty | 0 | 0 |

2008, budgetary restraints forced us to move that cap to twenty-five.

Thanks to strong administrative leadership, RU has invested heavily in information technology. In terms of access to technology, the majority of our 500+ sections of first-year composition courses are taught in "semi-smart classrooms"—that is, classrooms that have a networked computer, a computer projection system, a document camera, and a DVD player. Back in 2007, RU loaded document cameras, projectors, and computers in nearly all classrooms. As a result, our FYC instructors can easily project student writing on a large screen, show online videos, and showcase academic resources. Our composition teachers are of the first YouTube generation, often showing clips or using the Internet to spur classroom discussions. Additionally—from just about anywhere on our growing campus—students can access the wireless network. We are wired. Armed with an iPad or some other wireless device, students can use the campus networks from anywhere on campus, even in their cars.

Thanks to this rich array of information technology resources, we have high expectations for our faculty.[2] Our instructors must complete the university's technology requirements—to record first-day attendance, midterm grades, and final grades in Blackboard—as well as FYC's own set of requirements—to respond to student email, complete My Reviewers (the FYC online writing assessment rubric), and upload course documents such as detailed teaching schedules and office hours to our FYC website. Each FYC instructor is required to respond to three drafts for each of the three major writing projects in each class—at least 198 responses in a typical class of twenty-two students. In addition to major projects, instructors are required to assign at least two in-class essays, weekly blogs, and additional homework assignments. All of this student work requires instructor feedback.

During the first two years of our effort to provide instructors with peer-production tools to collaborate in our effort to develop a shared pedagogy, we received no special funding from RU. We had no money to purchase or support servers and no funds for a server administrator's time. Therefore, we had to find funding from various sources, the most significant of which has come from the university General Education Council's approval of our proposal for a mentoring program.

### INTERACTING FACE TO FACE:
### THE MENTORING PROGRAM

As Clark Campbell reiterates in "Best Practices for Student–Faculty Mentoring Programs," "Mentoring has been an integral part of education from the beginning of academia. Plato learned at the feet of Socrates in what could be described as a mentoring relationship" (326). And while mentoring has drastically changed from this classical Greek relationship, close mentoring relationships between faculty and students are still going strong. "Virtually all" institutions of higher learning initiate mentoring programs to help students make graduation day, indoctrinate graduates into the professional realms of publishing, or pass down valuable teaching skills (Campbell). Regardless of this gain in popularity, standardized mentoring programs do not exist. Over a decade ago, Maryann Jacobi wondered whether the only common thread of multifarious mentoring programs was the desire to help someone else (505); other than that, mentoring programs vary so much that it's hard to draw connecting lines between any of them. Despite any clear leadership about how best to "do mentoring," we wanted to jump into the fray; our incoming teachers deserved it.

In a proposal to RU's General Education Council in 2006, we noted that we "did not have the necessary resources to mentor instructors who are struggling or to teach our students to use new communication technologies." We lacked "funding to test-pilot the benefits of new teaching models such as co-teaching efforts or online efforts" and "the necessary funding to conduct a thorough assessment of what is working and what is not." In summation, we argued that we lacked "the funds for program necessities: to keep the existing program websites working as well as funds to develop these websites to better meet our needs" and to "continue what has proved to be a remarkably successful online teaching evaluation process." We proposed to use the funds for seventeen course releases for outstanding FYC teachers to continue assessment efforts and to integrate our assessment effort with our mentoring effort, as well as to support new staffing needs for an associate director, a mentoring director, a website coordinator/community manager, and an assessment programmer. FYC staff intended to use mentors as a catalyst for developing teaching strategies, planning and enacting program assessment, and creating a collaborative community.

Our proposal was successful, and mentors have taken an increasingly crucial role in our program. The mentoring program has allowed graduate students, instructors, and adjuncts the opportunity to work with the director of composition to publish a writing program philosophy, generate new projects, prepare a programwide online assessment tool, standardize subjective grading in order to lower grade inflation, produce ENC 1101 and 1102 textbooks used by all FYC students, and update the program website to fit the curricular modifications. We've also used mentoring funds to enhance professional development and allow instructor voices to be heard: mentors and facilitators interview FYC staff, host pedagogy workshops, and initiate mandatory FYC meetings throughout the academic year. The hope is that these efforts will help to create a community of instructors. To accomplish these tasks, we choose mentors based on their effective teaching skills rather than on their technological proclivity. At times (especially in our early days) this meant choosing mentors who were hostile to technology, yet we believed we needed to focus on selecting the "best" teachers, and we also assumed we could acclimate these teachers to technology— that we could mentor the mentors. Plus, as we explain in more detail in Chapter 5, we believed we needed to provide space for critique, dissension, and underlife (Brooke defines *underlife* as "those behaviors which undercut the roles expected of participants in a situation—the ways an employee, for example, shows she is not just an employee, but has a more complex personality outside that role" [141]). The mentoring program contributed to the creation of a more cohesive community by connecting administrators with returning and incoming teachers. The goal of the mentoring program was to add an extra layer of collaboration in addition to our use of social software and peer-production tools, but both initiatives were designed to create community among our quickly revolving population of instructors.

## SHAREPOINT AND INSTRUCTORS' TECHNOLOGY USE

To best explain the context of our research, we briefly describe some of the common and uncommon ways that our instructors are able to use peer-production tools to shape their own teaching experiences and the trajectory of the program as a whole. Our description of these tools should not be read as if we uncritically proclaim them to have effected agency among our teachers; however, we do see these as methods that have affected our teaching context considerably. Many of these tools are based on our main website, which ran Microsoft Office SharePoint Server 2007 when we conducted this study—and which, in the face of budgetary difficulties, we've been pressed to use creatively in a number of different contexts, ways that Microsoft may never have imagined.[3]

### SharePoint at RU

One of the best aspects of SharePoint is its permissions features, which allow each aspect of the site to be visible and/or editable by different groups of people, including anonymous viewers. For instance, parts of our site are password-protected so that only instructors and administrators can view them, while others are editable by instructors; some sections can be edited by a registered instructor or student, and others have selective permissions for specified small groups. This ability to share with the outside world (including built-in RSS feeds for every page, document library, or list) is one of the chief benefits of this software for our program, especially for graduate students wishing to share with colleagues and hiring committees.

Yet despite our excitement about SharePoint's power and flexibility, many of our instructors found the 2007 SharePoint interface too difficult to master. Although the FYC staff developed simplified video and printable tutorials on how to do the most basic tasks—say, adding a link or a document to an existing list—the architecture and overall usability still tended to intimidate some users. Much of this was our fault as Web administrators, since we shaped SharePoint in ways that best fit our community's needs as opposed to what would be easiest to build. For instance, much of our page content was created in blank webpages and then fed into the SharePoint interface via inline frames to decrease the chance that unwitting users would accidentally delete crucial material. If we had used the wiki tools or the simple rich text editor Web Part, the site would have been easier to use, but in the first year of our implementation we lost a good deal of content when one of the users erased our rich text editor Web Part, not realizing there wasn't a backup version for this content in SharePoint 2007.[4] User error has also been an ongoing problem, as our instructors report confusion stemming from minor issues such as trying to return to earlier pages with their browser's back button (a function that is never permitted in database-driven websites), clicking a list title and finding themselves in an unexpected interface, or finding problems when using their College of Arts and Sciences password, which requires resetting about once a semester and which many instructors rarely use and thus forget.

Most of our pages are Web Part Pages, made up of individual Web Parts that are created individually before being fed into the Web Part Page (see Figure 2.1). The Web Part concept gives us a way to display diverse pieces of information such as Web links, lists, events, database queries, and external webpages onto a single page with dynamic page updating. Lists of relevant documents stored in a document library can be updated by a content manager from the Web Part while immediately updating the document list wherever it is displayed. Thus, much of the Web development process used at other major websites is unnecessary, since the content editor Web Part provides a rich text designer, and Web Parts for libraries and lists are automatically created for the content manager. Similarly, automatic creation of input forms for custom lists, document modification alerts by email, user-targeted views of lists,

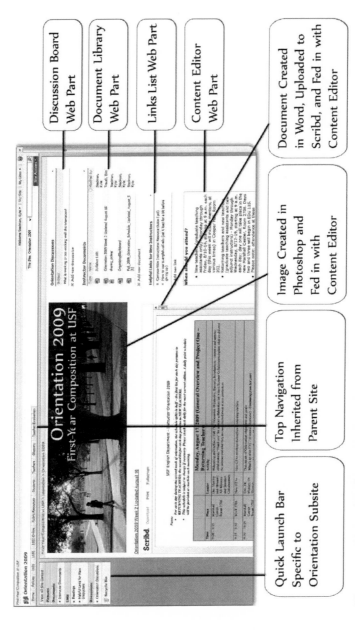

Figure 2.1. Typical Web Part Page in SharePoint

and automatic survey results pages also make it easier to develop highly functional interactive webpages. We often used FrontPage and then SharePoint Designer to create customized webpages when this functionality was desired.

The complexity required in administering this kind of functionality could become quite intimidating, which may explain why some users were hesitant, or even hostile. Another difficulty we encountered was the fact that the Microsoft Campus Agreement license at RU between 2004 and 2010 did not include students—just faculty and staff. While this was no problem for our instructors, it did prevent us from moving forward on one of our primary goals: student collaboration on document development, forums tied to projects, and embedded blog and wiki parts. This was frustrating, since one of the major reasons for choosing SharePoint was that we hoped to implement a single sign-on so RU students could use their RU Internet IDs. Because we were unable to implement a single sign-on until 2010, we could not teach our students collaborative document development in the same system that our faculty and administration were using to accomplish that very task. Because students couldn't use the blog and wiki Web Parts in the first version of SharePoint, we needed to maintain separate systems for those tasks.[5]

*FYC Instructors Using Online Tools*

A short description of a few of the technologies our instructors rely on will better contextualize the spaces where we collaborate—and fail to collaborate—online.

- **Teaching Community:** During fall 2007, some instructors requested a password-protected site to share content that might not be suitable for student viewing. This request led to the development of our Teaching Community (TC) site, which hosts various wikis for teaching resources, assessment documents, and a colleague tracker feature, which encourages instructors to share resources simply by allowing access to detailed weekly schedules and successful (or failed) lesson plans. This SharePoint site encourages instructors to share documents and advice, participate in a teachers-only wiki, and create a profile to use as a home base for professional interactions with other instructors and (if they choose to adjust their privacy settings) with students and the rest of the world. Instructors are required to upload a copy of their syllabus, detailed schedule, and office hours each semester, allowing the FYC staff and fellow instructors to see what pedagogies have been working well for their colleagues and to know when they can expect to find their colleagues in their offices.

- **Instructor Links:** The most popular part of the password-protected TC site, instructor links offer a space for instructors to share project-specific lesson plans. Pages on our main, public site often include an "instructor link" button, which directs users to a password-protected page on the TC site. Designed for instructors, these pages contain multiple spaces for instructors to upload documents, share links, or discusss how they taught a particular assignment.[6]

- **Listserv:** Like many other organizations, our writing program has a high-traffic listserv (hosted by our university). Though our listserv precedes and differs from peer-production technology, it's a central tool used by our faculty, and it often impinges on our use of tools such as SharePoint or our wikis. Teachers will often upload material to our sites, then use the listserv to notify others of the recent contribution, or they will discuss the content of our site on the listserv, which acts as a complement to our peer-production technologies. Many of our instructors find the listserv to be the easiest way to share articles, Web resources, and lesson plans with the community. As with any listserv, of course, this ease of use comes with the attendant cost of unorganized material floating into over-crowded inboxes, never to be seen again—which led to the creation of the following tool.

- **Web Parts:** The SharePoint software supports a variety of customizable lists and document libraries called Web Parts, as they can be moved around part by part on the screen of many SharePoint-created pages (Figure 2.1). One of our main uses of Web Parts is to stack a number of them on the side of each of the essay assignment pages, with different lists available for different kinds of content (e.g., sample student texts, video links, print books and articles; see Figure 2.2). When instructors have something to share, FYC staff encourage them to find the appropriate Web Part on the appropriate assignment page. Once logged in, any writing instructor or WPA can add documents and links to these Web Parts, providing an ever-growing, community-driven, dynamic space adjacent to the fixed text of the essay assignment.

- **Colleague Tracker:** This subsection to the TC site generates a colleague list that includes updates to blogs or new material, including updates to office hours or any new uploaded documents. Allowing access into instructors' password-protected sites encourages information sharing and (hopefully) helps build community.[7]

- **My Site:** This personalized site is automatically created for every instructor with permission to access the TC site. It allows instructors to build protected or publicly viewable sites that use the available SharePoint features, such as organized, customizable links lists, documents, calendars, subsites, specific-purpose wikis, and so on. Some instructors use this site to build resources for other classes as well.

- **Wiki Glossary:** Our writing program staff faced a dilemma when defining unfamiliar rhetorical terms for undergraduate students: on the one hand, we wanted to ensure a clear definition with a focus on the angles that students would most need to know when composing in our program; on the other hand, we wanted to continue in the spirit of our instructor-led pedagogy—and a list of definitions can easily begin to feel monolithic, top-down. The answer came with our wiki glossary, a wiki page that lists common terms and encourages instructors (who all have editing access after logging in) to revise existing definitions, add links to helpful resources, or begin new links.

**Project Documents**                                              ▾

| Type | Name | ○ Modified By |
|---|---|---|
| 📄 | What does an annotated bibliography look like | Stedman, Kyle |
| 📄 | 1101Project1Rubric | Mitchell, Taylor |

⊞ Add new document

**Videos**                                                         ▾

▫ Rebecca Fiedler, "Using EndNote to Create an Annotated Bibliography"

⊞ Add new link

**Podcasts**                                                       ▾

▫ Duggan Library "Creating an Annotated Bibliography"

⊞ Add new link

**Websites**                                                       ▾

▫ The OWL at Purdue, "Annotated Bibliographies"
▫ Cornell U Library, "How to Prepare an Annotated Bibliography"
▫ Sample: Cinderella Romance Novels
▫ Sample: Martial Arts
▫ Sample: Interactive Fiction Scholarship

⊞ Add new link

**Books and Articles**                                             ▾

▫ James L. Harner, On Compiling an Annotated Bibliography

⊞ Add new link

**Research Resources**                                             ▾

▫ Craig Gibson, "Finding, Validating, and Annotating Web Resources"
▫ How to Write an Annotated Bibliography
▫ Citation Links
▫ USF Library Resource Page
▫ Crap Detection 101, Howard Rheingold

⊞ Add new link

**Sample Student Texts**                                           ▾

| Type | Name | ○ Modified By |
|---|---|---|
| 📄 | Wesley Crusher | Mitchell, Taylor |

⊞ Add new document

Figure 2.2. Sample Web Parts

Each word in the glossary can be linked to from various pages on our websites.

- **Wiki:** Additionally, we have hosted a number of wiki sites: writingwiki.org and teachingwiki.org were sites that a number of instructors used to encourage student-to-student communication (at writingwiki) and teacher-to-student communication (at teachingwiki). We also host a rather unstructured community wiki on our SharePoint page that all password-bearing members of the writing community can edit for various purposes, including sharing advice on how to interpret and use our program's rubric and repositories for sharing files and links that might be helpful to other instructors. At the time of this writing, this setup almost always means that only writing instructors and staff edit the wiki, but our plan is to open up this space for more collaborative work in the future.

These tools and others constitute the roads connecting different areas of our network. This network, constrained by our broader knowledge ecology—an ecology that shapes us by providing a certain budget, institutional context, and professional context—is informed by the innovations and ideas of each graduate student, adjunct, visiting professor, and administrator. We employ peer-production technologies in conjunction with our face-to-face interactions to constantly develop our curriculum. Over the past six years, our context has changed in substantive ways. Thanks to mentoring program funding, many of our instructors have assumed roles with greater agency—greater ownership and leadership of the program. Our curriculum is no longer defined by a single WPA, but negotiated from online discussions and open meetings. Some of our instructors have become activists, writing textbooks for our curriculum, pedagogical theory books, and online curricula and developing new projects. Thus, our research begins by questioning why all FYC instructors do not take more active roles and how, in the age of peer production, agency can be assumed by instructors housed in an underfunded and undervalued program. Our institutional and technological contexts structured our research study.

## METHODOLOGY

### A Note on Our Methodological Stance

Our study is qualitative, a close cousin to the methods used in ethnography and action research. Unlike the traditional ethnographer, who is outside of his or her community of study, we speak as insiders who have a vested interest in our findings. As Ruth Behar describes in "Ethnography in a Time of Blurred Genres," we purposefully "insert our participating and observing selves" into the research project (150). Of course, we understand there are problems with this rhetorical stance—observing but *caring*, never quite detaching—but we have come to see it as valuable. Traditional ethnography, rooted in anthropology, assumes a researcher must lack intimacy with subjects to have credible insights about them. Instead, we follow the qualitative-research-from-within approach of recent work in rhetoric and composition (Tinberg; Chiseri-Strater; Kutz and Roskelly; Durst; Ellis and Bochner). This includes Katherine Kelleher Sohn's personal investigation of the literacy practices of some of her former students at an Appalachian university and Lee Ann Carroll's longitudinal study of students' writing at her own university. Our study, like Sohn's and Carroll's, is similar to the "naturalistic inquiry" described by Yvonna S. Lincoln and Egon G. Guba, a methodology opposed to positivist assumptions. Lincoln and Guba remind us of the benefits that can come from the interaction between researchers and participants: *"Purposeful sampling and emergent design are impossible to achieve without interaction"* (102; italics in original). As writing program staff studying our teaching population, our interaction with our research participants is both realistic and unavoidable. Furthermore, we draw from Patricia Sullivan and James E. Porter, who call for "a postmodern empiricism that recognizes more fully the role of power in the research enterprise and that acknowledges as valid the political and ethical relations between researcher and researched; the rhetorical situatedness of all research activity; and the institutional constraints under which research proceeds" (xii–xiii). In short, we engage with our research participants by unashamedly interacting with them to better our program and investigate the various interactions between individual and collective power.

This action-oriented methodology often leads to the nonrandom selection of participants, as it did for us. Nonrandomness is unavoidable in qualitative research like ours, when we so-well know the participants. Like Renato Rosaldo in *Culture and Truth: The Remaking of Social Analysis*, we believe that as embedded researchers we are "somewhat impartial and somewhat partisan, somewhat innocent and somewhat complicit" (qtd. in Mitchell 9–10). One recent example of these *somewhat*s playing out in the context of participant selection is David Foster's comparative study of writing in German and US universities through the in-depth case studies of five students at two sample universities. He declares early on that his point is not to show how these students "typify the diverse populations of all American and German students and institutions"; instead, he wants "to illuminate significant elements of each system" (7). In this way, our study follows in Foster's footsteps. We recognize that our sample choices would not satisfy a statistician seeking to make widely generalizable claims within a distinctly defined margin of error. Instead, like Foster, we specifically sought people who would help us "illuminate significant elements" as defined by our experience and judgment. Foster reminds us, "What case study researchers seek is not distance nor detachment but the development of a holistic, personal interpretation of the evidence" (43). We believe this sense of personalized interpretation flows through Chapters 3, 4, and 5 of this book, where we specifically discuss our findings. And like Foster, we are content with a relatively small *N* (details to follow in Chapter 3), since the results we seek are humanistic and inspirational, not positivistic or statistical.

*Overview of Our Research Methods*

Our data come from three primary sources: archival research, face-to-face interviews with current teachers, and email exchanges with instructors—sometimes through focused emails to targeted individuals, and on two occasions through broader emails to larger lists. Our archival research at times reaches back to fall 2003, when Joe

Moxley became the director of composition. These data include texts found in past emails sent on our FYC listserv, surveys sent to instructors and students, analyses of our website activity, and writing program documents (e.g., rubrics, instructor contracts). Our data from interviews and recent emails, on the other hand, were collected specifically to help answer our research questions. This process, continuing on and off between May 2009 and February 2010, changed shape necessarily as responses forced us to consider new questions and new directions for research. The interviews usually lasted between thirty minutes and an hour and were discussion oriented; subjects (our instructors) were encouraged to go "off script," interpreting our questions as broadly as needed.

Our sample choices of subjects emerged from our roles in the writing program. After all, a book researched and written collaboratively between four authors can offer a broader sense of a teaching community than could one written through a narrower lens. In early discussions, we decided that we wanted to choose people for interviews who represent diversities of position (graduate students, adjuncts, visiting instructors), years teaching in the program, area of study (literature, rhetoric and composition, creative writing), level of education (working on or completed MA, MFA, or PhD), level of engagement in the program (e.g., those who always or never participate), and level of interest and experience with technology. For some of these traits, it's easy to identify instructors fitting a given profile, but for others, a mix of quantitative and personal data was necessary to help us find the widest variety of voices. For example, an individual's level of engagement with the program can be measured quantitatively through the number of times she logs in at the FYC website, the number of pedagogical materials she shares online, and the number of training and social events she attends—but her engagement can also be measured, though less precisely, by the impression she gives her colleagues about her attitude toward and excitement about FYC initiatives.

We're proud of our ability to pool these personal observations from a number of different angles to give us a complex sample group. Joe Moxley, as the program's lead administrator, was especially cognizant of budgetary needs, the program's history, and its relationship within the university's larger administrative bureaucracy. Taylor Mitchell and Quentin Vieregge both arrived as PhD students in fall 2006, but they still came from different angles of knowledge about which colleagues to interview due to their different roles (Taylor as mentoring coordinator and Quentin as research assistant to the director of composition), areas of study (Taylor as a literature student and Quentin as a rhetoric and composition student), and areas of focus in the FYC program (Taylor as an organizer and motivator, Quentin as a computer expert and website manager). Kyle Stedman arrived as a doctoral student in rhetoric and composition in fall 2007, giving him the added dimension of closer relationships with those who entered at the same time and, as a program facilitator and community manager, giving him access to the technology needs and frustrations of a number of colleagues.

We identified thirty-one teachers in the program we wanted to talk to about one or more of our three main areas of inquiry: (1) their opinions on our standardized rubric, (2) their role as contributors to the program (via technology and other means), and (3) their opinions on our mentoring program. This number represents about 36 percent of our total instructors, a number that changes each semester; in fall 2009, for example, composition courses were taught by eighty-five instructors. Of these thirty-one, we eventually conducted face-to-face or detailed email interviews with twenty-six individuals, with some individuals contributing to only one area of focus and some contributing to two or three. These twenty-six individuals, we believe, voice a wide variety of the thoughts held by various individuals in our program. They include adjuncts, visiting instructors, and graduate students studying literature, creative writing, or rhetoric and composition in our MA, MFA, or PhD programs; they are also diverse in their opinions about the paper and online versions of our rubric, their experiences contributing to the program through technology, and their relationships with the mentoring program.[8]

Another response to our evolving research questions was the decision to send two emails to broad audiences with updated versions of our research questions. Because our initial interviews began in May 2009, at the end of the spring semester, our interviewees did not include any incoming fall 2009 instructors. During our extended research, we had the opportunity to gather responses from all twenty of the students taking the required teaching practicum in fall 2009; we received six substantive replies. And in February 2010, we also sent a brief set of open-ended questions to the entire FYC listserv about how and why individuals contributed to the program; we received thirteen substantive responses. Of course, some of these responses to email blasts came from people we had already spoken to, either in interviews or in a previous broad email survey; thus, in addition to the twenty-six already identified, we received data from thirteen additional unique new people from our two mass emails (a combined 46 percent of all instructors in a semester when eighty-five individuals taught). Following IRB guidelines, we have assured all participants full anonymity: all names are pseudonyms except when we refer to ourselves, and we occasionally change small biographical details to make individuals in our community unrecognizable even to readers who teach in our program. When it does not impede the meaning of our descriptions, we have changed the gender of some of our subjects to protect their anonymity. We did not systematically share our writing with subjects, especially given the number of instructors and our constant revision process. We did share our writing with instructors whenever requested. We used follow-up emails after many of our face-to-face interviews to clarify any confusion or unanswered questions and made certain to keep the agenda and direction of interviews open-ended and improvisational. Through these efforts during the interview period, we tried to clarify any misunderstandings or misrepresentations.

Finally, we have also scoured our programmatic archival data (again, with IRB approval) in search of relevant information to help us characterize our teaching community. These archival data include formal program assessment results, mentor exit interviews, and other qualitative data such as online surveys given to all our teachers about their preferences for program changes, as well as questionnaires filled out by teachers hoping to work for our program. We also dipped at times into the mid- and end-of-semester surveys administered to the thousands of students enrolled in first-year composition courses each semester. We usually receive a response rate of approximately 1,200 students. These surveys help us characterize students' perceptions of our rubric (both paper and online), our overall curriculum strategies, our textbook choices, and various other concerns. In short, our archival data are in some ways our "best" data due to the large numbers of people surveyed since 2004, though it is of course also least targeted to the goals of this project. We therefore rarely rely on it.

## RESEARCH QUESTIONS

In brief, this study examines what motivates or dissuades instructors from authoring a shared curriculum in a large university writing program. We use archival, survey, ethnographic, and case study methods to find answers to the following questions:

- How can our first-year composition program use peer-production technologies and face-to-face faculty development efforts to create a shared pedagogy that focuses on specific, shared outcomes?
- How can we balance our shared pedagogy with our instructors' need for individual agency? How can we use our shared pedagogy to create a communal agency?
- How can we extrapolate open-source and peer-production technology core values to use as a foundation for a curriculum?
- How do face-to-face relationships influence online relationships, and vice versa?
- How do we create a "gift culture" that draws the best out of both those most willing to give and those more reluctant?

## CONCLUSION

While we can point to some successes (e.g., increased participation in curriculum design), we nonetheless acknowledge that we have been less successful than we aspire. We hear rumblings among our teachers that only a select few really drive the program. We see that few teachers go online to suggest readings, videos, or instructional activities. Even though we are inspired by outside scholarship, we still find many of our teachers fearful of technology, collaboration, and dialogue. We wonder how we can better inspire the gift-giving nature of Wikipedia and other collaborative sites.

In the spirit of wanting to throw a great party, to embrace our teachers and students in a shared collaborative effort to construct the best possible learning community, we wonder what we should stop doing, what we should continue doing, and what we should do instead. Having identified the literature that inspires us and acknowledged the budgetary context that shapes us and at times silences us—and obscures our vision—we interviewed willing colleagues and searched through our archives to revise our understanding of effective pedagogical communities. With this research to inform us, we are beginning the effort of moving forward from this moment.

We believe our results will be of special interest to writing program directors who want to use social media to rethink pedagogy. More broadly, we think our results provide a qualitative response to the hyperbole driving a good many social media articles. And at the national level, we believe our results affirm the incredible talent and commitment of graduate students and adjuncts as faculty—faculty who are not merely holding the hands of the academically adrift as they age (Arum and Roksa), but faculty who sit down with students, listen to them, and do whatever is necessary to help these students move forward as they walk into our classrooms.

## NOTES

1. Some of these students are counted twice, as everyone is required to take both ENC 1101 and ENC 1102 unless they test out or have advanced high school credits. Our unique student count is approximately 4,000. This number reflects a significant decrease from five years ago, a decrease that can be traced to RU's ever-hardening academic standards.

2. We recognize it may not be commonplace to call graduate students "faculty," but such is our stance when we submit emails or talk about our community.

3. In summer 2010, we upgraded to SharePoint 2010 and subsequently created a new site from scratch, using many of the same basic design features but with a number of tweaks. We also changed Web addresses, from http://collegewriting.us to http://fyc.usf.edu. This change came at an awkward time for this study, but the context of our interviews remains firmly the context of the old site and its organization. When appropriate, we note how something has changed on the new site.

4. Our pages on the new site, using SharePoint 2010, are almost all built with wiki pages, which have always included versioning but which now include many much-improved and dynamic page layout options.

5. From recent funding, we purchased the site licenses that have allowed students to author on our site since spring 2011.

6. On the new site, we've moved away from the password-protected TC model, instead sending all "instructor link" buttons to a public area of the site that's primarily for instructors and where this kind of collaboration can still happen.

7. The colleague tracker proved unpopular, and we haven't continued using it on the new site.

8. As naturally happens, our early interviews led to shifts in the questions we focused on in later interviews, as intriguing possibilities we hadn't considered before arose. For example, in research about our mentoring program, our initial discussions with individuals consisted of questioning how the mentoring program builds community or offers agency. But the responses we received led us to focus increasingly on specifics such as the connections between mentoring and the practical actions that teachers take (or do not take) to share their pedagogical materials with others. Similarly, our interviews about contributions to the writing program initially focused largely on asking instructors to self-identify the roles they take in the program; responses to these questions led to exploring the extent to which individuals created and distributed new writing projects. What became our chapter on the culture of assessment (Chapter 3) began with a specific focus—the online rubric tool—that eventually broadened into an examination of the wider implications of a program-enforced, standardized grading tool in general.

# 3

## Creating a Culture of Assessment

*How has the age of peer production changed assessment practices? With a community of teachers so different in expectations and experience, to what extent is it possible to use technology and face-to-face interactions to create a culture of assessment that seeps into every area of teaching? How does a tool such as My Reviewers reconfigure the authority of the writing program administrator, teacher, and student? And perhaps most important, how can writing program administrators share power by crowdsourcing the development of assessment tools?*

ONE WAY TO ILLUSTRATE THE relationship between assessment and agency in a writing program is to consider how writing programs such as the one we have here at Research University are similar to and different from a large professional orchestra. Our FYC program can be compared to a large orchestra with strings, woodwinds, brass, percussion, and so on. In an orchestra, each group of instruments is unique in its purpose, sound, and contribution, but each group or part needs to be in harmony with the whole. Just as the woodwind section needs to fit in with the strings, first- and second-semester composition courses need to follow each other without students missing a beat between semesters or feeling an unseemly rupture in the synchronicity of the curriculum. This is obviously the ideal, if not the everyday practice. And to keep the symmetry of sound in motion, an orchestra needs a director to coordinate, to provide feedback, and to, well, orchestrate. So too the writing program. But this comparison falls flat like a bad note in a few respects. First, composition programs are a bit messier than this comparison would imply. Teachers are always trying new lesson plans, innovating based off of existing writing prompts, or responding to the specific needs of their students. Whereas an orchestra performs together in real time, a program's faculty work together asynchronously, each faculty member with different talents, different students, and a slightly different context to work within. The messiness of first-year composition—which is to say the individuation of teaching from section to section—is how many new ideas, writing prompts, and pedagogies are formed, and teacher agency is strongly associated with this messiness.

Teachers and administrators both highly value that type of individual agency, but it coexists alongside institutional agency. First- and second-semester first-year composition are two of the few courses that most students at Research University enroll in, and students in these courses come from multiple disciplines, backgrounds, majors, and even year levels (an occasional junior or senior can be found on the class rolls). These courses draw the attention of university administrators because of the program's scope and size. A shared curriculum combined with excellence in teaching—demonstrated in part through attention to programmatic assessment of student writing—improves the reputation of the program, which in turn provides the material conditions that allow teachers the freedom they value in the classroom. Therein lies the problem: how to provide a consistent and reliable learning experience for students while still respecting the agency of instructors; how to find a way of interlocking these two goals and to express to teachers the relationship between institutional and individual agency. As WPAs we have responded to this need for a shared curriculum by creating an online assessment tool, which we now call My Reviewers, http://myreviewers.com.

The online assessment tool became operational in fall 2008 and has been a pioneering effort at RU as the school prepares for its reaccreditation. From its humble beginnings, the online rubric tool now allows for student–peer review, instant notification of teacher feedback, analysis of student improvement between drafts, and the aggregation of grading data, including everything from plotting grade differences between sections and instructors to averaging out the most frequent teacher comments. While we are experiencing great support and energy surrounding the tool, with other departments expressing interest in using it for writing intensive Gordon Rule courses, our growing success with the tool has traveled a rocky and winding path—often an uphill climb with moments of Everest-like intensity. Our story about how we began that process and what we have learned about the need for assessment and the variance of administrative and instructor perspectives follows. Earlier we mentioned that peer production has worked like an earthquake, transforming society, education, economics, and the making of knowledge. Yet like other major transformations grounded in technology, these changes are not always initially welcomed.

## ORIENTATION 2008

"You're requiring us to do what?"

The teachers in the room weren't happy. When the mentoring director had hopped on the stage to lead that afternoon's workshop, she was prepared for some resistance to upcoming curricular and technological changes—but not hostility. Gathered in a large, dark auditorium on the first afternoon of the fall 2008 orientation were mostly graduate students, with a few adjuncts and visiting instructors sprinkled in—a total of about forty people. While the new instructors were in another workshop elsewhere on campus, Taylor's job as mentoring director was to discuss the new, required online rubric tool with returning instructors. And with Joe Moxley away moving his daughter into her dorm, the job of explaining the changes fell to Taylor. Moxley had warned her that the requirement for all teachers to use the common rubric would be deeply unpopular, but she had told him not to worry. She was, after all, one of them: she could win them over! After two years working with FYC, Taylor knew instructors' names and the majority of their concerns. She even thought that if she were up there on stage instead of Moxley, instructors would be more inclined to hold an honest discussion about the new assessment protocol. She was right about that at least. After some introductory explanations, she announced without hesitation, "So now, for the last draft of each project—*just the last draft*—we are going to be using the new, required online rubric tool." The crowd didn't hesitate either; the tone of the room quickly grew cloudy: "Did she just say *online* and *required*?"

The conversation that ensued outlasted the afternoon workshop, spread virally on the listserv, and seeped into office discussions. The dirty *R* word was everywhere, and this incident sparked a widespread discussion about our culture of assessment. But to be clear, this incident cannot be analyzed in isolation from the larger context, because the effort to implement programwide assessment was just the latest episode in a four-year endeavor. The writing program had been fighting financial obstacles and revising assessment strategies since 2004, when we instituted our first required rubric with the goal of offering more consistency in essay grading across sections of composition. Since 2005, instructors' employment contracts had mentioned that at least the final draft of each of the three major writing projects needed to be graded using this official FYC assessment form. Though some instructors graded on word processors by typing scores and comments into digital copies of the forms, most instructors filled the rubrics out by hand, printing their own or grabbing a handful from a ready stack in the department mail room. So the announcement was a continuation of the program's policy, but it was completely new in that it required instructors to score student essays from an online website, which sent an email link to the student and to a database where administrators could access it.

"What is the least amount of time I have to spend with this new rubric?" asked Peg, an older adjunct who had been teaching longer than the current director's tenure as WPA.

"Are you asking about how to satisfy this new requirement?" Taylor responded, unsure of how much wiggle room to give instructors. Thanks to a WPA preparation meeting earlier in the week, she knew the bottom line—instructors must input the scores for each rubric category into the tool's Web interface when grading the final draft of the semesters' three writing projects. But Peg's question highlighted for the group the amount of extra time an adjunct with three sections would have to spend with the new rubric—three classes capped at twenty-two students, three projects per semester, at least 66 rubric screens per class equaled 198 online rubrics for the three sections Peg taught. Other comments heard during the orientation indicated confusion, frustration, and resistance:

- "I like to take a stack of papers to Barnes & Noble so I can get *away* from the computer every once in a while. Just because some people want to stare at the screen all day doesn't mean that I want to."
- "We're required to respond in some way to three drafts of each of the three major writing projects, right? For a total of nine total responses per semester? So how often do I need to use the rubric, then?"
- "I hate being stuck to my desk."
- "I can't type as fast as I can handwrite comments."
- "I need to proofread every line of my students' work. Have you seen how bad some of this writing is?"
- "This is just another example of the program changing things every year."

Frustrated laughs erupted when a senior adjunct professor loudly said to her neighbor, "Great. So it's like Big Brother is watching over us." This wouldn't be the last time Big Brother was mentioned. The next day a returning adjunct instructor sent an email to the program director with his satirical newsletter, the *Orientation Observer*, attached, subtitled "A Big Brother Publication" (Figure 3.1). The *Observer* included an article about Moxley's daughter's move to college, "I Chose Duke Because They Promised 'No Rubrics,'" which begins:

> Having seen the toll the Great Rubric Controversy had on her father, Dr. Moxley's daughter felt compelled to offer some further insights into the matter: "I was originally going to go to Research University, but one evening I came home and there were all sorts of gnomish-looking people standing around Dad's desk chanting 'Rubric . . . Rubric . . . Rubric!' When they saw me, they started shrieking 'Interloper! Interloper!', but Dad calmed them down and reassured them that I did indeed belong in the house."

A Big Brother Publication

# Orientation Observer

Volume 1, Issue 1                 August 18, 2008

*Let's Meet the Newcomers*

- "There WILL be discipline in my classroom."

- "I like to be loose and creative in the classroom. After all, 'All work and no play...'."

- "I'm going with the latest in technology in getting my class to click. How do you like my new digital SLR camera?"

## FYC Coup— Kim Makes Her Move

"I believe that the old adage 'While the cat's away...' still has some clout," chuckles Kim.

"With Joe gone up north, I can maneuver a whole batch of new TAs and Adjuncts—and perhaps sway a few of the returnees—to become my counter insurgency."

"My main strategy to seize control will be to place the Rubric blame on Joe. I'll let a tear roll down my cheek as an emotional appeal, and I'll let my years of service vouch for my credibility. Finally, I'll stun them all with the cold, hard logic of the necessity for the overthrow."

"I'm going to take the program in a radical new direction. Why waste our time teaching students who can't tell the difference between a dangling and a squinting modifier? Why teach surly louts who spend the class periods IMing their friends?"

"Instead, we'll be spending the entire semester holding orientation sessions and getting free lunches from publishers. We will truly be a moveable feast. Let's keep orientating till we get it right! Now, who's with me?"

## Rookie FYCers Show Quick Progress

After just one week of intros and orientation, the 2008 class of FYC TAs and Adjuncts show a dexterity that their more veteran colleagues can only marvel at.

"I've not seen a group so capably balance the info and instruction since the legendary class of 2002. But even those TAs couldn't master this structure of technology, the strength of grammar avoidance, the inherent agility of wikis and blogs. This group truly is setting a new ideal."

**Figure 3.1. An instructor's satirical newsletter mocking changes in FYC assessment protocol**

A few days later, Kyle, then technology coordinator for the program, sent an email to the instructor listserv with some poems focused around the word *rubric*, which he explained as being inspired by the newsletter. Interestingly, this email doesn't mention the controversy at all, beginning simply with a lighthearted, "A couple of us were trying to think of what rhymes with *rubric*, just in case we ever write a song about the FYC program." The email thread took off, and over the next twenty-four hours, nine people sent their own rubric-based poems through the list, including students in rhetoric and composition, literature, and creative writing, and students who were new TAs, returning TAs, PhD students, MA students, MFA students, and one librarian—but no adjuncts. A representative sample:

> I once taught a student named Kubrick,
> who turned in a draft about two bricks.
> 'Twas boring and sad,
> so boy was I glad

> An instructor who'd so far eschewed tricks
> to win him to FYC rubrics
> Greeted the new one with elation;
> said "To build a foundation,
> one always must start with two bricks."

> So much of a grade
> depends upon
> a red marking
> pen
> informed by a rubric
> beside the white chickens

> You say there's no rhyming with "rubric"?
> The OED Online's no true brick.
> Its search box is awesome!
> My poem will blossom
> And end with a line slick and lubric.

After the initial email's avoidance of the topic, it was especially interesting to see how some of these poets played with the negativity of the initial meeting by briefly adopting the role of critic before quickly stepping away. For instance, the third poem sent out came with both a poem and a disclaimer:

> When I first heard the news, I almost got sick:
> I'm forced to use yet another rubric!
> I mean, who is this dick? Yes, whom shall I kick?
> I then learned 'twas not one, no many had won;
> Collab'ration, it seemed, had got this thing done,
> So I cursed the rubric AND its authors, those pricks!
>
> Y'all know if I REALLY cared one way or the other, I'd have been rather vocal on it at Orientation! Bad words just happen to rhyme in this case. . . .

This ambivalent tone continued in other poems: one author explicitly labeled one poem as "POSITIVE," in which the speaker "could show [a poor writer] why [his essay failed] with my rubric," and another as "NEGATIVE," in which the speaker "was told that I had to use this damn rubric." Only one haiku was written: "'Rubrics are no fun!' / This might be the death of me / Please kill us now; please!!"—but it was immediately followed with ". . . Only kidding. Have a nice weekend."

### THE WPA VIEW ON ASSESSMENT

So how did we get here? What was our rationale for requiring our teachers to use an online rubric to evaluate students' writing and critical thinking? How did we get from our overall mission—of creating a community of teacher-scholars united in a shared effort to prepare first-year students for academic writing—to these disputes about using an online rubric tool to respond to students' writing? What had inspired us to believe that we could employ new social media tools and database technologies to develop a robust teaching and learning environment that better met the needs of our students and teachers? Lacking a budget and coding skills, had we somehow gone down the wrong avenue? As we explain in the following section, we were guided by institutional and external pressures, by research and scholarship, and by the teachers' ongoing resistance from 2003 to 2007 to a paper copy of the rubric.

### Why? External Pressures on the Writing Program

Assessment depends, in part, on the program's relationship to larger stakeholder groups, such as the student body, regulatory agencies such as the Southern Association of Colleges and Schools (SACS), the university, surrounding schools, and other writing programs across the country. Back in 2008, as we completed the first version of our online rubric tool, our writing program was feeling a good deal of strain as a consequence of SACS reaccreditation, the national recession, and a series of academic setbacks for Florida universities. Most important, a former satellite campus was reprimanded twice by the SACS Commission on Colleges, in December 2007 and June 2008; the second reprimand put the satellite campus on a one-year probation in part because of its failure to assess "the academic skill of general education students, in areas like writing and critical thinking" (Matus). A local newspaper aptly described the dense thicket that RU and its satellite campuses were about to experience as "particularly thorny" because "it plays into a simmering national debate about measuring student progress in higher education. And it has been a tough nut to crack for many institutions" (Matus). Indeed, leaving nothing to chance, our main campus of RU underwent a major initiative to strengthen every aspect of its assessment. Each department was tasked with rethinking its assessment practices, and the university's Office of Assessment was restructured as the Office of Institutional Effectiveness, chaired by a newly created associate vice president position—which shows the importance RU has given assessment efforts recently. We were also mindful that the state's flagship university had lost its composition program, and we feared the same would happen to us unless we improved our assessment results.

All of this happened during a time of record budget cuts across the state and the beginning of the greatest economic recession since the Great Depression. Every university in our state faced massive budget cuts, and only the three largest (RU included) were allowed to offset their loss in revenue with steep rises in tuition (Lewis). In his state of the department address, our chair warned us that our department would be fighting for every dollar—and, indeed, by 2011, RU had lost 100 million dollars from its operating budget. When placed within this context, it's clear why the agency of the writing program was so important; it is not an overstatement to say that we faced an existential threat from accrediting agencies, legislators, and probing university administrators asking whether we really deserved the limited funding the school had to spare. But though our instructors knew that the university was undergoing massive budget cuts, they may not have understood the connection between these problems and the institution of My Reviewers.

### Why? Theory and Research

Writing assessment has always been a thorny issue for English studies. As just about any student has discovered, different teachers have different standards for grading. Research has repeatedly demonstrated the unreliability of teachers' grades (Diederich; Breland; Moxley, "Responding," "Teachers'"; Sommers; Elbow, "Ranking"), leading some theorists to argue that teachers should abandon altogether the practice of ranking and grading. Peter Elbow is perhaps the most well-known and respected critic of contemporary grading practices, arguing:

> We can sometimes get agreement among readers from some subset, a particular community that has developed a strong set of common values, perhaps *one* English department or *one* writing program. But what is the value of such a rare agreement? It tells us nothing about how readers from other English departments or writing programs will judge—much less how readers from other domains will judge. (Elbow, "Ranking" 189)

Elbow acknowledges "some large overlaps" ("Do We Need" 88) in agreement across discourse communities, yet he faults efforts to train groups to grade in similar ways: "It is always a story of power being deployed" (84) because "to 'calibrate' readers . . . means forcing them to check their own values at the door" (88).

In addition to demonstrating the difficulties writing teachers have ranking and grading papers objectively, research has demonstrated that teachers need to improve their ways of responding to student writing. Poor grammar and mechanics sway readers' judgments of other factors such as the quality of the critical thinking or research (Rezaei and Lovorn; Scannell and Marshall; Charney). Even nonpertinent issues such as gender or the attractiveness of a student's looks has been found to sway teachers' comments (Malouff). Nancy Sommers's 1982 article "Responding to Student Writing" highlights teachers' struggles to provide quality feedback. Sommers observes a few core problems instructors have when providing commentary, such as not differentiating between surface-level and content-level issues. Sommers's findings have been confirmed many times by similar studies. For example, in their 1993 study of 3,000 papers, Robert J. Connors and Andrea A. Lunsford found that 23 percent of the teachers' comments were negative: "These completely critical comments ranged from savagely indignant to sadly resigned, but all gave the message that the teacher was seriously disappointed" (210). More recently, in a 2006 follow-up to the Connor and Lunsford study that looked at students' evaluations of 498 graded papers from "hundreds of courses from 30 different departments in the university" (22), Lesa A. Stern and Amanda Solomon found that most faculty "comments were technical corrections that addressed spelling, grammar, word choice, and missing words" (22); comments about "organization and quality of the ideas" were "surprisingly absent" (22).

Kathleen Blake Yancey describes assessment in writing studies as being like a series of three overlapping waves, with newer waves not erasing older ones but coming alongside them and drawing some focus away from them (Yancey, "Looking Back" 483): the first wave was objective testing, the second holistically scored essays, and the third portfolio assessment. Years later she updated her focus on the assessment of student outcomes with the addition of a fourth wave: a focus on programmatic assessment, not just assessing students or student outcomes (Yancey, "[Still] Historicizing Assessment"). Yancey's framework is especially useful to this study because of the ways our assessment strategies attempt to affect the day-to-day culture of teaching, assess student outcomes, and assess our program at the same time. We are trying to ride that fourth wave of assessment through the aggregation of teacher–student commentary online. By aggregating the thousands of responses of teachers to students' texts, as opposed to randomly selecting a few hundred papers for holistic scoring, we are bringing this fourth wave to new heights as only recently made possible by database computing.

Clearly, though, research in assessment and teacher feedback is quite murky, including the timeless problems teachers have providing objective feedback and the faults associated with teachers' tendency to emphasize superficial errors even when rubrics give more grade weight to more global concerns, such as the use of textual evidence. Therefore, we realized that our online rubric tool was unlikely to be a magical resource, one that transcended the difficulties teachers have had or that researchers have tracked. These difficulties, such as inter-rater reliability, have been traced in the research to as early as 1912 (Starch and Elliott). Rather than design a single rubric that would be applied to the six major projects in ENC 1101 and ENC 1102, we realized the importance of eventually designing the rubric tool so that it allowed users to design their own rubrics or adjust template rubrics. That said, for now we could see many advantages to using one rubric to assess all academic writing. Conceivably, by using a single scale to assess academic essays, the online rubric tool could be used not only in first-year composition but throughout general education—indeed, throughout a student's university education—to track the student's development of critical thinking and writing skills. Furthermore, by using the same rubric, scores within each course could be compared to one another more meaningfully.

In fact, while we embraced Elbow's argument on a theoretical level and recognized that different readers may employ different criteria to measure the quality of texts, we ultimately believed that Elbow was overstating the subjective nature of assessment. At this point in time (although Graff hadn't yet written "Why Assessment?"), we felt that it was an injustice to students to follow Elbow to the logical conclusion of his argument—that any objective assessment is an impossibility and that academics across disciplines don't share any core values. We worried that Elbow's position was the sort of isolationist, compartmentalized thinking that was ultimately undermining education. The extreme position that all faculty hold different criteria would lead instructor commentary into a wasteland. As representatives of thousands of students every year, we believed we owed it to our students to define the overall characteristics of academic writing that would be expected of them throughout their college careers. And, yes, we believed it was possible to identify the principles of writing—such as organization or research—that academics at RU tend to share. Instead of assuming that it was impossible to provide objective feedback by developing a single rubric to assess student writing, we hoped to give teachers and students a common vocabulary to discuss academic writing in ENC 1101 and ENC 1102. Plus, by assigning grading weights to the criteria, we hoped to establish some standardization among the seventy to eighty instructors who teach in the program each year. These efforts were meant to circumvent idiosyncratic grading in which, for example, poor basic grammar or word-level errors disproportionately determined a reviewer's overall grade.

By developing our online rubric tool, we hoped to bring clarity and transparency to our grading criteria, even if the establishment of these criteria represented increased power of writing program staff. Additionally, in time, by engaging teachers and students in ongoing developments of the rubric criteria and the tool, we hoped to soften the imposition of will on the individual. Bottom line, perhaps—as pragmatists—we thought we owed it to our students to clearly define our grading practices. We were also influenced by the pioneering work of Fred Kemp and Susan Lang at Texas Tech who in 2002 began using a form of distributed assessment, with papers and comments organized online (Kemp). Kemp and Lang responded to the problem of grading inconsistency among instructors by applying new technological possibilities and a previously impossible grading organization: they created a networked database with a user-friendly and user-specific Web interface so that student essays could be graded by instructors who were not their classroom instructors. This method created a double-blind grading mechanism that reduced the possibility of bias. The problem of grading inconsistency and inflation was addressed by having each paper graded by at least two instructors. Our own efforts followed Kemp and Lang's inspirational example of using a common online rubric across sections of the same course. However, cognizant of our teachers' concerns with their own agency in the classroom, we have avoided using document instructors, preferring to keep the grading within the hands of the classroom instructor alone.

Nonetheless, despite these challenges, we believed it was important to start somewhere, even if it was a point of departure. Given our lack of a budget during the early years of our effort, we embraced Elbow's concept of "playing the believing game" (*Embracing*), and like a writer who looks at a "shitty first draft" (Lamott 21), we gave ourselves room to dive deep into the drafting of the rubric tool.

### *Why? The Writing Program's Assessment History*

When Joe Moxley became director of composition in 2003, he wanted each FYC instructor to use CLAQWA to evaluate students' major projects. CLAQWA was an eighteen-point analytic scale developed by Terry Flateby, director of assessment at RU, and Elizabeth Metzger, an associate professor of English. Moxley reasoned that it made sense for teachers to use the CLAQWA rubric because the university was using it to assess writing and critical thinking in both the writing program and the general education program. He hoped making the CLAQWA assessment criteria transparent would help our community move in the right direction.

From 2003 to 2008, the Office of Assessment continued using CLAQWA to assess the writing program. But, based on teacher feedback, it quickly became apparent that CLAQWA's eighteen-point scale was too detailed for routine classroom use. As a result,

Joe and colleagues worked to crowdsource the language of the rubric tool, the definition of grading criteria, and materials the teachers developed so as to help instructors better understand the rubric and use it.[1] By 2008 the rubric contained six major sections: Focus and Organization, Critical Thinking and Support, Use and Integration of Sources, Style and Language, Grammar and Mechanics, and Format.

However, after five years of requiring the use of a shared paper rubric to assess student work, students' mid-semester surveys and end-of-semester teacher evaluations indicated that many of the instructors were not using the rubric. The surveys suggested that although instructors were *required* to use the FYC rubric, many students had not actually seen it. In fall 2007 and spring 2008, just before the online rubric tool was first unveiled in fall 2008, FYC students were asked to take an end-of-semester survey, which included the following question: "The Writing Program asks instructors to use the FYC Assessment Form at least once in response to three major projects. Did you find this form useful or should we discontinue its use?" We received 912 responses. The five options (six, if you count leaving the question blank) seem, in hindsight, more ambiguous than they ought to be (see Figure 3.2)—a lesson we have learned each semester when we return to the survey questions from the previous semesters and struggle with the desire to clarify their language and to see how responses to the same questions change over time. Still, these numbers do indicate that in the 2007–08 school year, as many as 36 percent of the students were not exposed to the "required" rubric, if we add up the percentage of those surveyed who did not see it (9 percent), didn't know what it was (20 percent), and left the question blank (7 percent). If we add the 17 percent of respondents who replied "Not sure," which could indicate either "I'm not sure if I find it useful" or "I'm not sure what you're talking about," the number of students not familiar with the rubric could jump to as much as 53 percent of respondents—though it could also be as low as 29 percent, if we add the 20 percent who responded "I don't know what the FYC Assessment Form is" to the 9 percent who responded "Did not see it." Regard-

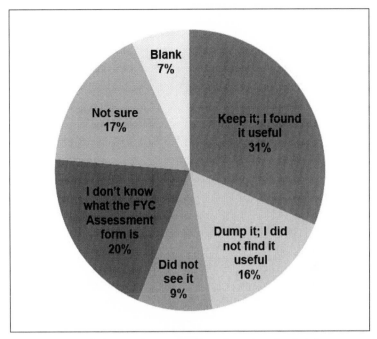

**Figure 3.2. Student responses regarding the printed rubric's usefulness, fall 2007 and spring 2008**

less of which percentage is more accurate, our assessment practices clearly needed to change.

As a result, Joe decided to require use of an online version of the rubric tool. In part, then, surveillance was intentionally embedded into the architecture of My Reviewers. And in requiring use of the tool, Joe recognized he was—to use Joseph Nye's metaphor—moving partially from a governing ethos of "soft power," which involves persuasion, to one of "hard power," which involves coercion. The relationship between hard power and soft power concerning the rubric was complex, however. While telling teachers they could change the rubric—its language and pedagogical support materials—or change any other aspect of the writing program so long as the changes received communal support, Joe was valuing power based on rhetoric and persuasion. Change was a consequence of ideas, rhetoric, and even charisma rather than coercion, fear, or even violence. Soft power was the underbelly of our curriculum development and mentoring program. But when it came to *requiring use* of the rubric tool, we took a harder, hierarchical stance. We were engaged—as least the writing program director was—in hard power. By moving from paper to an online version of the rubric tool, the agency of the writing program was significantly enhanced: use of the rubric tool by teachers to evaluate student work could easily be tracked—and assessed. The tool enabled a writing program director or researcher to access the tool to determine how an individual instructor's grade distribution differed from the norm. Given that the tool aggregated teachers' comments, it provided a window into the historically closed discussions between teacher and student.

During the early days of developing My Reviewers, Joe wrote, "We need to figure out how to harness the incredible creative energy of teachers and students to dialogue about learning practices. I believe that if we do not assert our right to design and develop our own datagogies, we will concede the central pedagogical stage of the 21st century" (Moxley, "Datagogies" 200). In his proposals for funding and notes to users, Joe advocated numerous advantages to the online rubric tool. He was especially excited about the ways My Reviewers could close the gap between what had traditionally been called "formative assessment" (ongoing assessment, the sort teachers provide when students are allowed to revise) and "summative assessment" (the kind of assessment historically done at the conclusion of the semester, after the students have left the building). Rather than conducting an after-the-fact assessment—a process whereby ten instructors read 5 percent of our student population's texts—My Reviewers provided real-time assessment information: if, for example, 3,000 students in ENC 1101 were not showing improvement on a rubric criteria—say, "Use and Integration of Sources"—the writing program could immediately revise its shared curriculum to give more instruction in information literacy practices. In this way, Joe hoped to close the loop on traditional assessment practices, to cojoin summative evaluations with facilitative evaluations. In addition, he believed teachers could benefit from knowing how their scores compared with the scores of other teachers. For example, if an instructor assigned mostly As while the group mean was mostly Bs, the classroom teacher would benefit from knowing that he or she was an outlier in terms of grading.

My Reviewers presented possibilities for both research and programmatic improvement. It could enable administrators, teachers, or students to track progress on a single measure across time or a collection of measures. Students and teachers could track their progress or lack thereof from draft to draft, project to project. We would be able to compare growth from project to project and semester to semester. From project to project, or between our first and second composition courses, we could measure the difference between student successes on different writing criteria. We could see which projects were most or least demanding. This database could serve as a valid archive to research the validity of student complaints or to spot a wide disparity in grading patterns between instructors. Ideally, given the time and the inclination, research could be done on a massive scale about what types of written commentary worked best. My Reviewers would do all of this by harnessing the grading strategies of more than seventy teachers and, with luck, improve instructors' responses as a result of research on this aggregated data, as well as by allowing teachers to generate reports that enabled them to run comparisons of their grading practices with those of their colleagues. (See Figure 3.3 for the spring 2009 version of the rubric.)

### A CAUTIONARY NOTE: BUILDING
### A HOVERCRAFT IN THE WATER

Before sharing our teachers' more individual responses to our deployment of the first version of My Reviewers, we should pause for a moment to give some background information about our technology ecology. While developing our online rubric tool, we often felt as though we were building a hovercraft in the water: our tool was unleashed with only quick, informal testing among staff members instead of going through a thorough beta testing phase, a decision that was often debated in staff meetings. When challenged, Joe

## Writing Assessment Rubric

| Student Data | Course Data | Instructor Data |
|---|---|---|
| Name: | Term: Spring | Date: 5/24/ |
| Email: | Course: Select course.. | Name: Kyle Stedman |
| Status: | Project # Select project... | Email: kstedman@ |
| Last Modified: | | |

*Select course data; then select student*

<u>Click here for more information about the rubric.</u>

| Save | Send Email |

**Focus and Organization**

- Addresses **audience and purpose** appropriately for the context.
- Provides an effective **opening** and **closing**.
- Sustains main idea through a **logical** progression of supporting points and provides necessary **transitional language**.
- Discusses each idea to the extent **appropriate for the essay's audience**, resisting the urge to stray.
- Includes paragraphs **unified** around a topic related to the main idea.

of 100 pts.
(20% of grade)

**Critical Thinking and Support**

- Develops **interesting, sophisticated, and reasonable ideas**
- Critically analyzes **relationships** between ideas.
- Avoids **overgeneralizations**.
- Uses purposeful details to **support and develop the thesis**; the mere inclusion of details is insufficient
- Provides the reasoning necessary to be **persuasive** (when appropriate to the assignment)

of 100 pts.
(20% of grade)

**Use and Integration of Sources**

- **Selects and integrates sources** in ways that are appropriate to the genre of writing
- Uses and assesses **credible source material**
- Appropriately uses **primary and/or secondary research**
- Skillfully integrates sources in quotations, summaries, and paraphrases (when required) that:

| | | |
|---|---|---|
| a. | Support student writer's focus **(not used as filler)** | d. Are **carefully integrated** into writer's voice, not excessively quoted, with block quotations used sparingly and appropriately |
| b. | Are **reputable** and appropriate | |

of 100 pts.
(20% of grade)

**Figure 3.3. Rubric tool in spring 2009**

joked that this was the Google way, that we had to learn by doing, that we couldn't wait a year until the following orientation—the one time our community gathers collectively each year.

We should also acknowledge that this first version of My Reviewers was constructed on a shoestring budget—basically by an act of will by Joe and his friend Terry Beavers, who at that time worked for RU's IT department. Regrettably, IT preferred that Beavers not take on consulting positions, and he was warned not to work on FYC materials during work hours. Given this context, it is perhaps not surprising that we encountered numerous parts of the tool that weren't working correctly, such as the tool timing out and erasing teacher comments. The erasure was actually an unintended side effect of an IT security policy that assumed teachers would not need more than twenty minutes to grade a student paper. Some students reported never receiving the emails sent to them with their grades and commentary, most likely a function of spam folders and email filters. At times the online rubric was offline or the site took an excessive amount of time to upload. And as anyone responding to technical difficulties knows, it was often difficult to ascertain whether the problems arose from coding issues or from user issues. After all, we had one instructor who had trouble with the suggestion "Double click your mouse." "What mouse?" she asked. "I don't see a mouse."

Because the program lacked an inhouse IT designer, during the first year of My Reviewers implementation Quentin became an unintentional liaison/detective trying to diagnose his fellow teachers' complaints and concerns about the rubric. As the author of the step-by-step instructions and introductory instructional videos on how to use the rubric, he was daily approached in person or via email whenever anyone had a problem with it. Insofar as these complaints were a result of confusion about how to use the tool or why, this was an easy and fulfilling task. But oftentimes, what at first appeared to be user error turned out to be a coding problem, a task more appropriate for the website's designer. Since our IT designer was working on the rubric as an after-hours project, Quentin emailed him only when it was finally clear that the problem wasn't user error. But coming to this conclusion often took a great deal of time. The origins of a problem could only be recognized inductively with each additional piece of information, each additional frustration or complaint. This led to some complicated but inevitable conversations; emails became daisy chains between multiple instructors, designers, and administrators. Since these early days, however, we've streamlined communication problems and hired an inhouse Web designer.

### INSTRUCTOR VIEWPOINTS

But enough of our perspective; let's dive into the viewpoints of our instructors about the online rubric. (A note on the following section: we've let our instructors' voices be heard without immediate response or analysis; we then close the chapter with some thoughts about the overlap or distancing between administrator opinions and instructor opinions.)

Juliet, a long-time adjunct instructor, described in an interview her desire for more customization of program requirements for different instructors, with a focus on how to balance standardization and instructor agency in grading. She didn't think our program's goal should be to achieve "cookie-cutter classes, because instructors come from different backgrounds, experiences, and contributions; therefore they can bring to their classes different strengths and outlooks." Along these lines, she pointed out that the FYC program's standard outcomes and student writing projects give enough standardization to the program; she felt that taking the next step of requiring everyone to use the same rubric crossed the line. Juliet went on to explain the conflict between her personal preferences to grade solely on paper and our program's computer-driven pedagogies:

> I'm a hands-on grader, preferring to mark on the students' printed papers. One of the suggestions for revising is for the students to print a draft of the essay and read it out loud, marking on that copy and then make changes. If everything becomes strictly online, students will most likely skip that suggestion. I would not like it when/if the comments become required [i.e., typing comments into the online rubric tool] because that would mean double duty for me. I do not like to be constantly tethered to the computer because it bothers my eyes after a while, and it is just a tool and not a "be all to end all."

Juliet packs a number of different issues into this response: her fear that students' revision will falter without her hands-on, read-aloud approach; her belief that students are more likely to skip revision strategies that are computer based; her insistence that typing comments into the rubric tool would be "double duty" for her; and an especially intriguing final statement of frustration about computers being seen as the "be all to end all" by some—presumably including Joe, an avowed technorhetorician who constantly challenges our writing program to include new technologies (e.g., blogs, wikis, podcasts) and websites. Juliet's responses clearly indicate that she takes assessment seriously, both as a reader of her students' work and as a teacher who encourages them to learn the transferable skill of reading aloud as a new way to read and assess their own work. In some ways, then, she views the coming of the rubric tool as an infringement on her personal commitment to assessment.

Sonya, another long-time adjunct instructor, explored the computerization of writing assessment in her interview, with a healthy dose of frustration mixed with some praise. In her nine years of teaching at RU, she had grown comfortable with the rubric itself (though she is frustrated by the online tool), so much that it has ingrained itself in her regular practices. In an email, she wrote:

> Interestingly enough, I now also teach at a university which doesn't require a rubric at all, and I seem to have the RU rubric planted in my head when I grade. Although grading without a rubric is less "quantifiable," I think that the grades land in the same "ball park" they would have been in had I used a paper or online rubric. It's the rubric training that counts, in my humble opinion. What I'm getting at, in a roundabout way, is the fact that a rubric is a rubric is a rubric. It matters not to me whether a rubric is on paper or online or in my head, I just need to use one in order to grade my students in any fair or consistent manner, and this fact is probably due to my RU training, for which I am grateful.

In other words, the rubric itself isn't what's important—it's the shift in mindset, the mental training to read essays for preset criteria in order to be as fair as possible. In this framework, the rubric seems both crucial as a starting point and inconsequential as it becomes part of her "assessment" mind. The online tool, however, forces Sonya to confront multiple distractions that can pull her focus away from her task, seemingly making it harder to achieve the zone she needs to access the rubric inscribed on her mind; Sonya described the inherent distraction of sitting in front of a computer, the "tech glitches" that can come from the rubric tool or Blackboard, and the possibility that her own computer or ISP will decide to act up.

Sonya did have a small praise for the rubric tool: its ability to get grades to students for the final project of the semester—which, even if graded in a frenzy, often can only be returned to students by hand if they get around to dropping by their instructor's office to pick up the graded, commented version. "Now," Sonya wrote in a follow-up email, "the students can receive a detailed rubric online, helping them to understand why they received the grade they did and also to know what they did well and what still needs improvement." Her praise is all for the practical side, for what the tool can offer her students. But still, she asked, "This additional requirement is going to take up more of my time, and for what?" Why, in other words, should she be expected to adapt to a new system that requires her to sit in front of the computer for hours? To her the rubric tool seemed like an unnecessary quirk, a technological blip that she was happy to do without.

### Panopticons and the Problem of Privacy

Much of the concern surrounding our online rubric tool can be traced to strong beliefs about the nature of privacy. Our instructors, when asked to use an online tool to communicate private information in an educational context, felt pressed by their conflicting understandings of and goals for their professional lives, teaching development, and students. Though the online tool was developed in conversation with university counsel to ensure that it follows FERPA guidelines for student privacy, teachers still expressed uncertainty about how much privacy they were entitled to when it comes to the details of the grades they give students, when each score and comment inputted into an online form is stored in a database. "Big Brother" was mentioned in the satirical orientation newsletter in fall 2008, but the phrase also came up in interviews with two of our instructors for this project, as did the suggestion that the rubric tool represents a sort of panopticon, Jeremy Bentham's famous prison design that would allow prisoners to be watched at all times. To what extent can or should administrators have unfettered access to the detailed grades and comments that instructors give to their students? And does that answer change when the administrator is a writing program administrator, college dean, or university vice president? And how would the digitalization of assessment information impinge on FERPA and access to information? These questions inform this project's conversation about instructor agency in a large writing program, as instructors' technical/legal concerns blend with affective concerns. How much power do instructors feel they have when they submit grades and comments both to their students and to an electronic database?

In the case of visiting instructor Dominic, issues of electronic privacy were at the front of his mind when grading with the electronic rubric. His interview was notable for his quiet fear about how and when his grades and comments potentially might be used against him. He said, "I am still a little bit wary about the fact that the grades get sent to the boss, and they get sent to people in the English department, and that the grades become public to a certain degree." In many ways, his responses remind us that the rubric tool collects two overlapping kinds of data: the grades and comments the *students earned*, but also the grades and comments the *teachers assigned*. The rubric is designed to assess how well students are attaining the clearly stated outcomes of the program, but it seemed to Dominic that the rubric also assessed how well teachers were attaining a hidden standard of grading that *hadn't* been clearly stated—whether too high or too low, too many comments or too few. Dominic explained that this fear of being watched hurts the ability of the community to work together—which is a critical point, given that the collection of so much grading data in some ways represents a digital community, if not a culture, acting together toward the same ends. "I think that ultimately," Dominic explained, "having your grades emailed upstairs is almost counter to, runs almost counter to this idea of community. It also makes me feel like there's people that I *can* talk to about the rubric and people that I can't talk to."

Dominic's fear of public knowledge of grades should have been alleviated by communications from WPAs, but his persisting concern demonstrates how hard it is to disseminate information in a large program. Furthermore, his fear has a distinctly technological angle to it, especially when he says, "I type the numbers in; I don't *know* where that data goes." The act of inputting grades seems to feel similar to inputting private information in any blog or social networking profile: users have an inkling of who may access the information, but they have often been warned to err on the side of caution, given the fact that once something is put on the Web, it becomes accessible in unpredictable new ways. Despite the locked nature of our rubric data, and the secure settings for accessing the Web interface (an https site), perhaps the mere fact of inputting information through a Web browser feels antithetical to the carefulness many of our instructors have learned in their day-to-day Web literacy. But Dominic's instincts about the privacy of educational pursuits are also understandable—he wondered who would have access to information that only students should have access to, since he had probably been warned again and again throughout his teaching career to keep student data completely private. He was actually surprised that more people hadn't brought up this issue; he struggled to find a word other than *outrage* at what he thought people ought to be expressing. But he also told us that his girlfriend, who teaches at another university, "thinks it's a complete violation," and that she has "repeatedly" told him that she would never teach "in a program where they so closely monitor their teachers." Of course, the director and assistant director have always had access to the grades of all FYC program instructors, but they had never before been able to read the detailed comments given to each student or the grades given to each individual student on each individual assignment (at least not without considerable difficulty).

The online rubric tool also highlights the critical role of clear communication in efforts to build a culture of assessment that respects both collective and individual agency. A number of instructors expressed fear about the uses to which the collected data about instructors (e.g., number of papers graded, average scores) would be put—an intriguing turn, given that the program's purpose in collecting data was to gather *student* score data. Dominic wondered if the scores he gave students might come back to haunt him if he later asked for a letter of recommendation for another teaching job; he worried that overall memories of his teaching might be positive until a WPA cracked the file of rubric results to find that he had graded higher or lower than desired. Sonya mentioned, "Certainly the thought that we are being monitored is an incentive for conformity," a sentiment reflected more negatively when another instructor, Matthew, constantly repeated the word *panopticon* to describe the rubric tool: "Even if the rubric becomes properly 'enforced' through the department penalizing or firing teachers who do not use it, it is still little more than a panopticon to survey teachers' grading methods." Matthew, a doctoral student in literature with experience teaching at various area colleges, used the online rubric tentatively in fall 2008, though he used it more regularly in spring 2009. Like many instructors, he didn't announce his decision to stop using it in fall 2009; he simply chose to silently rebel, betting that nothing bad would come of it—a reaction different from Dominic's fear of retribution, perhaps due to Matthew's status at RU; he was there primarily for his doctoral studies, whereas Dominic was there primarily to teach. But despite his casual dropping of the tool, Matthew still saw it as an invasion of privacy. In his email interview regarding the assessment tool, Matthew wrote, "An all seeing eye, while effective at promoting standardization, also seems to be contrary to the program's philosophy and towards a revocation of teacher rights ala the patriot act, and also as many teachers feared when the rubric was first instituted."

These characterizations of the tool's purpose are due at least in part to communication gaps. In meetings with FYC staff, we understood the tool primarily as a way to collect data on the grades students earned, and not as a way to police the teachers by connecting those grades to individual teachers. We mentioned this approach in our *Appeals* newsletters and listserv emails, yet the message remained unclear. Instructors received our messages but didn't necessarily believe them. Despite our efforts at reassurance, some paranoia prevailed. And some fear was understandable. After all, while writing program directors have always received reports on their instructors' grading, never before has this information been provided in real time and never before have WPAs at RU been able to see so easily where individual instructors stand in relation to other instructors.

New tools worry teachers, so WPAs need to carefully consider how the tool is deployed and why. Otherwise, given the paranoia that can erupt when asked to change a time-honored grading practice—that is, scribbling in red ink on a page—teachers may misread an administrator's message. For example, in spring 2009, the second semester of the online rubric tool's implementation, Joe sent an email to all FYC faculty listing every instructor's name and the average grades they had given in each of six rubric categories, headed by, "If you do not see your name below and have been using the rubric, pls let me know asap." Joe's goal in sending this email was to inform the faculty that they were indeed expected to use the rubric and also to confirm that it was working as designed. Instead of nurturing the intended culture of assessment, however, the email inadvertently fostered a culture of fear. Suddenly, each instructor's aggregated grades were known to every other instructor; those who had not used the rubric were embarrassed because their names were not on the list of those who used the rubric. Moreover, some faculty disliked the transparency of this report; it made them feel as though they were being watched: some we spoke to were worried that their jobs in future semesters would depend on their adoption of the tool. From these reactions, we realized we needed to move from a culture of fear to a culture of information.

The transparency of today's database tools runs in some ways as a headwind for changes in perspectives of authority in our culture; Nye observes that "polls show that people today are less deferential to authority in organizations and politics" (1). We've certainly experienced the lack of deference and the willingness to question and be openly skeptical about administrative requirements through the process of implementing our online rubric. Instructor comments like Juliet's indicate a resistance that results from confusion about the purpose of the tool, a suspicion about how it will affect her professional reputation as an instructor, and a general resistance to change.

At the time of the "Big Brother" email, Joe realized that it might cause some consternation, that the posting of data reflected a move from soft power to hard power. At the same time, he felt the message was necessary because we were not getting the level of participation we expected or needed to conduct meaningful assessment of student work. For five years he had provided soft power encouragement to use the paper rubric, and survey results had demonstrated the rubric still was not being widely used. Therefore, as much as he worried that being forceful about using the online tool would undermine his effort to create a collaborative culture, it was a move he felt compelled to make. For Joe, the conundrum of balancing an emphasis on the gift culture and wielding necessary administrative power had no simple solution.

A final anecdote highlights the relationship between communication and instructor agency. Adjunct instructor Claire explained to us how she reacted to hearing that instructors would be required to use the online rubric to input scores for a minimum of six categories. Her actions highlight subtle ways that teachers can use their personalities to try to carve out spaces in which they can grade in the ways that make the most sense to them.

> Well, I went up to Dr. Moxley's office to tease with him because you know he sent us out the little quote-unquote "threats." [Laughs.] About how if we didn't use it we might not be hired next semester? And so I went into his office to tease with him about it and he just took on this persona of being so serious. All like, "Oh, no, Claire we all know that you are an excellent instructor, *but*, I don't want you to see this as my rubric, but as *our* rubric." And he just went into a depth of seriousness and I was like, "Okay Claire, you failed—your attempt to tease him failed, so let's go get the rubric done." [Laughs.]

Claire gave it her best shot, but Joe challenged her to see the big picture, to accept a sense of ownership over the rubric and thus to get on board and use it. In response, she laughed and returned to her office, failing in her power play and ready to use the rubric. But at least she had tried.

*Teacher Agency vs. Program Standardization*

Claire also told a story that echoed Sonya's praise of a rubric's ability to enforce a degree of standardization that wouldn't be possible without it. Her story, and those that follow, are instructive examples of a struggle that we believe many teachers experience, as do many individuals in any large organization: the tension between wanting to trust your gut as a knowledgeable professional and wanting to coordinate your actions with others in your organization. Despite Claire's attempt to avoid using the rubric tool, she praised the rubric language and the concept of a rubric as a tool of standardization, as did many of our teachers. She opened her interview by painting a picture of the rubric as a sort of boundary for graders who are liable to get so drawn into the topic of the essay that they lose the distance of the objective grader:

> Because when you're looking at a paper, sometimes the paper, the *stuff* gets interesting, and you get off *focus* because you say, "Wow." You know? "I didn't know that this percentage of women in Hillsborough County had been assaulted." You know? "I didn't know rape or homelessness was so prevalent in St. Pete. Oh, look at all these young people that are being killed in Miami!" And so you get off focus—you're supposed to be looking at also, how well did they cite this information? Have they over-cited the information? And do you hear their voice? You know what I'm saying? Because you're listening at all these examples that they've pulled out of their research, but in the midst of putting all these examples in, though they are interesting, the student's *voice* has gotten lost.

When instructors face this situation, which we can perhaps call the danger of liking an essay too much, the language of the rubric stands there like a fence, reminding instructors to respond just as they would to another essay that didn't draw them in as much. Of course, it's worth questioning just how much such distancing is possible or desirable in a grader, and it's worth questioning just what makes essays effective or ineffective, and in what blend. Still, Claire helps draw our attention to the possibilities a rubric can offer when a program needs to promise university officials and accrediting agencies that students across hundreds of sections are receiving a somewhat similar learning and assessment experience.

Matthew, however, offers an important counterpoint. He responded most energetically to our questions about the standardization potential of an online rubric. In an email, we asked him, "What do you think about the online rubric tool as a way to promote standardization across sections of composition classes? Or in a broader sense, to what extent do you think standardization is an important goal for our program, and what means ought to be taken to work towards it (if any)?" His response was clear:

> First off, I don't think the rubric effectively promotes standardization, at least not to any real extent that adds to this current format of our FYC program. Admittedly, having the rubric does indeed force individuals to conform to the department's standards of grading individual essays, but at the same time, that department standard is also already so clearly and fully publicized with the NUMEROUS sample assignments, handouts, and project designs available online that having the rubric just exist, and asking teachers to use it, doesn't do anything new.

Matthew seems to see the shared curriculum of our program as going far enough toward standardization efforts, with anything else pushing the envelope further than necessary. He described two reasons for his hesitation to use the required online assessment tool: first, he has the (admittedly poor) habit of procrastinating and getting all his grading done in last-minute chunks, which "did not lend itself to adding an extra component/added time consumption." Intriguingly, his second reason is that he doesn't trust himself to be brief when typing comments: he wrote in an email response to interview questions, "I have found that since I do not like my own handwriting it is easier to abbreviate my already copious comments when scribbling them, as compared to typing." This objection contrasts with the more typical computer complaints we heard—not wanting to stare at the screen all day, not wanting fingers and wrists to cramp up, etc.

Where to turn? From Claire and Sonya's perspectives, we should view a rubric's potential to help standardize a large writing program as a crucial tool, but Matthew, Dominic, and Juliet remind us to keep looking at its problematic implications. More important, these interviews reminded us of the disparity between instructors' and administrators' perspectives. Not only does each group have different answers, but at times we have different questions as well. As administrators, our questions have more to do with how the tool can create a shared curriculum and the practicalities of how it can be built with a limited budget and human resources. Instructor concerns have more to do with teacher autonomy and evaluation of effectiveness in the classroom. Still, the concerns of administrators and instructors are not mutually exclusive. What's needed are institutional mechanisms such as interviews, the mentoring program, online instructor questionnaires, brown-bag lunches, and our fall orientation, all of which help to foster dialogue. The experiences of Paulo, a doctoral student in literature, help to illustrate how that gap between perspectives can be bridged, specifically concerning our online rubric tool.

Though it's not the perfect answer, one approach to this conundrum grew out of Paulo's successful formation of a rubric subcommittee: our invitation to teachers to take an active role in shaping the standardizing forces. We believe that by authoring pedagogical and assessment documents, instructors can influence our FYC program to an extent not available at many other schools. Our first interactions with Paulo about the rubric, before this research project began, were not propitious. Paulo, who had completed his PhD course work and was then working on his literature dissertation, taught first-year composition for the first time in fall 2008, when the rubric tool was first unveiled. As someone with many years of experience in developing software in business contexts but relatively little experience with teaching writing, Paulo found the quirks of the rubric tool frustrating, especially because they hindered his efforts to better understand the ins and outs of writing assessment. At the same time, the more he thought about our rubric language, the more he found repetitious and unclear criteria—and this on a document that was meant, in part, to judge the organization and clarity of student writing. On more than one occasion, Paulo raised his voice in anger at rubric-related issues.

As the first semester of online tool use progressed, it became clear that Paulo could lead an effort to recommend beneficial changes to both the rubric tool and its language over the 2008–09 winter break. Joe invited Paulo to form a subcommittee that spent the end of fall 2008 putting together an extremely detailed report that served as the basis for the WPA's decisions about which changes to implement for spring 2009. Instead of complaining into the void, Paulo and the other instructors who worked on the rubric subcommittee stepped into a new role as shapers of the standardizing forces that were pressing on them. Having asserted his ability to help make the language of the rubric more effective, Paulo then asked us for a revised tool that empowered teachers to grade in ways that not only saved them time but also made their grading fairer and, in his words, more "meaningful"—which was, of course, our goal.

Regardless of his initial frustration and quite possibly due to his work on the subcommittee, Paulo's response to the rubric was perhaps the most balanced of our interviewees, mixing praise and criticism. His interview also stands out for his request for even more instructor agency through technological revisions. He told us, "I like the idea of a rubric. I like the idea of trying to get some . . . commonality in terms of, at least to a certain level, on even how we grade, or what is important. Because this way a program communicates what is the value of development versus language versus grammar—I think that's important." But like everyone else we spoke to, Paulo found the early technical problems with the online tool frustrating. "So I like the idea," he told us, "but I was frustrated with the execution." He reiterated that "the things you love are the biggest dangers. . . . Technology's always got to be a help, not an imposition, and figuring out that line is not easy."

Paulo dreamed of a user interface that displays much more of the data from the underlying database, allowing comparative scoring between different students and between the past and present scores a student has received. The transcript of his interview gives readers a sense of how excited Paulo was to explain this dream interface to us; his words and ideas rush together:

> When I found myself trying to really use the system, what I wanted to do is go through all my students in the class and look at each category and kind of preliminarily put up a number. And then I could look at it and say to myself, "Well, am I being fair? Is so-and-so really a thirteen and somebody a fifteen and somebody an eleven in this category?" . . . If I could pull up for a class, a number, like a spreadsheet, putting my numbers where I can argue and fiddle, and *then* go to individual sheets to put in comments—'cause it would avoid double work, and that's the way I grade; I don't know if other people do that or not, but, you know, again, let's just avoid—because it really *is* all comparative! There is no absolute "what's a fifteen," "what's a thirteen." But at least within a class I can push myself to try to be as fair as I can.

To Paulo, agency is access—access to the database, to the scores he has previously assigned, and more generally to the possibilities that he knows are inherent in database-driven computer applications. He sees grading as essentially comparative but questions how far the scope of that comparison should reach.

### RESULTS: THE WPA VIEW

As writing program administrators, we have learned a lot from the initial pushback, confusion, and critique that emerged from our teachers in response to the implementation of our online rubric tool. In Chapter 6, we discuss some of the lessons about communication and writing program administration that we learned from this experience, as well as our other efforts to peer-produce a shared, standardized curriculum. Without enumerating all of these lessons here, we would like to conclude this chapter by focusing on what we have learned related to scholarship on assessment and responding to student writing.

As you can imagine, we had assumed teachers would respond negatively when we required the use of My Reviewers to assess the final drafts of the three major projects in ENC 1101 and ENC 1102. After all, we knew that many teachers preferred the custom and simplicity of writing notes on student papers. Using version 1 of My Reviewers meant that our teachers had to log on with their Internet ID, view and respond to the papers online, and grade them using the required rubric. Nonetheless, we were surprised by much of the resistance and underlife we faced. Although we had intentionally designed some supervisory elements into the architecture of My Reviewers, in our presentations, discussions, emails, and newsletters to teachers we had assured them that we wouldn't drill down into the particulars of their classes unless we faced a student complaint. We pointed out that though we would check the archive to see if teachers were following the curriculum, our mid-semester surveys and final teaching evaluations already provided that data. In this way, we tried to reassure them that the process of supervising graduate students and adjuncts remained mostly unchanged. Given that the director and associate director of composition have their own research agendas and teaching schedules, we explained, we lacked the time—even if we had the inclination—to burrow into the archive to ferret out, for example, incidences of grade inflation. We also publicly acknowledged that we understood that our process-based curriculum (students rewrite papers three times in response to teacher feedback) leads to higher grades than do non-process-based models. Finally, by inviting teachers to help us develop the rubric—by revising it, building resources, and providing usability feedback on the interface (not to mention the invitation to coauthor our curriculum, as discussed in Chapters 4 and 5)—we believed we had given teachers sufficient opportunities for personal and communal agency.

By conducting this qualitative research, however, we have become more sensitive to how assessment issues touch the nerve of teacher agency with particular acuity. Juliet and Sonya saw the online rubric as power taken away from them, forcing them to grade in a way they didn't want to grade. Dominic and Matthew felt their ability to grade by trusting their own experience and intuition was being challenged by a power-draining panopticon. Claire used subtle conversations with her boss as a way to test the limits of her agency—limits that Paulo also tested, first through vocal complaints and later by submitting a detailed list of suggested changes generated by the subcommittee he assembled. Clearly, these teachers, and presumably others in our community, believe that the use of My Reviewers diminishes their sense of agency.

However, it would be naïve to assume that a tool such as My Reviewers *inevitably* diminishes the agency of instructors. All of the instructors have a choice, as exemplified by Paulo, to engage in the ongoing development of the tool. For the architects of My Reviewers, as explored somewhat in the following chapters, the online rubric interface enhanced their agency, their ability to affect the teaching and learning experiences of our 6,000 to 7,500 students every year.[2] Thanks to the ongoing efforts of dozens of instructors, we now have a rich array of pedagogical sources (e.g., sample marked-up papers, videos on using the rubric tool, exercises) to help students better understand our grading criteria.

Because this study took place before the implementation of peer review capabilities and document markup, our analysis of the ways the tool impinged on student agency is limited. Perhaps surprisingly given our review of the literature earlier in this chapter, we can report that students have been very satisfied with their instructors' feedback—both when we used the paper rubric and when we moved to the online rubric. In fact, there has been a slight increase in student satisfaction with instructor feedback since we moved to the online version. In student surveys from fall 2007 and spring 2009 (before and after the online rubric), results indicate a similar amount of satisfaction with teacher commentary. In 2007, in a sample size of 358 students, 86 percent either agreed or strongly agreed that their teachers provided them with "sufficient feed-back," and in spring 2010, 89 percent of 1,040 students agreed that "[their] instructor provides [them] with the feedback [they] need to improve as a writer." If anything, these two surveys suggest a slight improvement in student satisfaction with teacher commentary after the initiation of the rubric. Most students were happy with their teachers' grading and fewer were apathetic or "neutral" (from 10 percent to 6 percent). These statistical changes obviously don't prove a cause-and effect-relationship between our rubric and student satisfaction, a relationship we can't prove or disprove without much more data. But we are encouraged by these numbers, even if they are only marginally better.

For the writing program, the effect of My Reviewers on agency are less ambiguous: use of the online rubric tool has advanced the agency of the writing program in meaningful ways. First, by constructing a rich resource at http://fyc.usf.edu to clarify our grading criteria, the writing program has made its standards transparent to the university community. This has provided financial support that we otherwise would not have received, support that has now extended beyond the million dollar mark and allowed us to involve faculty outside of the FYC program. From the General Education Council, we received a unanimous vote of support for the tool. In various proposals to university leaders, we argued that My Reviewers would benefit writing-intensive courses as well as online courses that wanted a vehicle to support writing assessment and peer review. For these efforts, we also received letters of support from General Education, the Classroom Redesign Project, and Undergraduate Studies. With increased support, we argued, My Reviewers could even be adapted by other departments. These efforts to explain the relevance of our program and the potential of our assessment efforts resulted in considerable success: we were awarded $10,000 from our university's Center for 21st Century Teaching Excellence, $10,000 from the Office of Institutional Effectiveness, $10,000 from Undergraduate Studies in 2009, $81,000 from Tech Fee Funds in 2010, and, most recently, $231,273 from Tech Fee Funds in 2011. Additionally, from the General Education Council we have received $695,382 over the past five years. While we continue to develop and pilot test My Reviewers, we are now partnering with faculty outside of FYC, so ultimately the tool may affect not just the 6,000–7,500 students who enroll in FYC courses each year but also the 30,000 undergraduates who are enrolled annually on a branch campus and must take one writing-intensive course to graduate. Given the budget crisis, we do not believe we would have received this funding without proven successes, as our university must be selective about the programs it supports.

Beyond contributing to the university's larger mission of enhancing the critical thinking skills, information literacy skills, and writing abilities of all undergraduates, our analysis of instructors' aggregated comments and evaluations has led us to close the loop between assessment and curriculum revision. For example, when we analyzed 7,154 assessments (many with both grades and comments) from our fall 2008 pilot of My Reviewers, we often didn't see clear growth in student writing from project to project for Style, Language and Grammar, and Mechanics.[3] This led WPA staff to completely redesign how we scaffolded the three required projects in subsequent semesters and to increase the emphasis on grammar and style in our ENC 1101 curriculum. Then, in spring 2009, when we noticed that ENC 1101 students were receiving progressively worse scores on Use and Integration of Sources, we redesigned how we approached research in our curriculum. Finally, our most recent assessment has provided perhaps the most interesting and compelling results: our community has achieved broad consensus when evaluating student texts, which clearly is at the very heart of our endeavor. During our 2010 assessment of the writing program, following a calibration session during which eleven scorers reviewed random essays written by 249 students (that is, 5 percent of our population that year) who took both ENC 1101 and ENC 1102, we found 0.892 inter-rater agreement using Cronbach's alpha coefficient among scorers. While agreement between a small group of scorers isn't extraordinary (we've known since the 1980s that rubrics work!), what was unexpected was that when we compared the independent scorers' evaluations with those of the classroom instructors on the same student papers, *we found no statistical difference on five of the six rubric criteria.* When scoring for Focus (Written Language and Critical Thinking), Evidence (Critical Thinking), Organization (Written Language and Critical Thinking), Style (Critical Thinking), and Format, our classroom teachers' scores almost exactly matched those of the independent reviewers (see Table 3.1). The only category for which there was disagreement was Style/Written Language, which represents 5 percent of the overall grade. For that criterion, the classroom teachers were slightly tougher than the independent reviewers, a discrepancy tied perhaps to the training of the scorers, who were warned not to allow superficial errors to otherwise sway their judgments.

For a theorist such as Peter Elbow, our findings might suggest that we have reached a degree of consensus that demonstrates a pernicious degree of groupthink. Most likely, Elbow would point to a few of our interviews, particularly Dominic's, as evidence for his argument that rubrics undermine the authority of the classroom instructor. Perhaps he would even dismiss our seventy-plus teachers' ability to reach agreement on the ranking of student papers. After all, Elbow questions, "[W]hat is the value of such a rare agreement? It tells us nothing about how readers from other English departments or writing programs will judge—much less how readers from other domains will judge" (Elbow, "Ranking" 189). In response, we suggest there is terrific value to our community's ability to grade in such remarkably similar ways. Sure, we are willing to concede that individual teachers may lose some agency; however, by using social software, writing programs can counter this loss of agency by empowering all teachers with a say in the definition of rubric criteria, development of the interface of a tool such as My Reviewers, and development of rich pedagogical resources. Thus, for a dialogical writing program, agency at the individual level is a choice: working as a group, individuals can have more power than isolated teachers. Our results demonstrate that we have been able to work meaningfully as a group to define the qualities we value. Rather than creating groupthink, we believe we have constructed a learning environment that enables both teachers and students to better give and receive feedback.

Table 3.1. Comparison of Classroom Teachers and Independent Scorers by Skill and Total Weighted Score (N=249)*

| Criteria | Skill | Means | | | Means | | |
|---|---|---|---|---|---|---|---|
| | | Independent Scorer #1(x) | Classroom Teacher (y) | Difference between means (x-y) | Independent Scorer #2(x) | Classroom Teacher (y) | Difference between means (x-y) |
| 1. Focus | Written Language | 2.54 | 2.39 | 0.15 | 2.53 | 2.39 | 0.14 |
| | Critical Thinking | 2.12 | 2.19 | -0.07 | 2.22 | 2.19 | 0.03 |
| 2. Evidence | Critical Thinking | 1.96 | 2.13 | -0.17 | 2.13 | 2.13 | 0.00 |
| 3. Organization | Written Language | 2.35 | 2.24 | 0.11 | 2.42 | 2.24 | 0.18 |
| | Critical Thinking | 2.03 | 2.14 | -0.11 | 2.16 | 2.14 | 0.02 |
| 4. Style | Written Language | 2.44 | 2.22 | 0.22 | 2.56 | 2.22 | 0.34** |
| | Critical Thinking | 2.18 | 2.09 | 0.09 | 2.31 | 2.09 | 0.22 |
| 5. Format | | 2.32 | 2.33 | -0.01 | 2.38 | 2.33 | 0.05 |
| 6. Total Score (Weighted) | Written Language | 2.38 | 2.18 | 0.20 | 2.48 | 2.18 | 0.30** |
| | Critical Thinking | 2.06 | 2.18 | -0.12 | 2.20 | 2.18 | 0.02 |

* Total *N* excludes a student with missing data
** Statistically significant at 0.05 level

More important, in response to the challenge "What is the value of such a rare agreement?" we could point to our students' satisfaction with their teachers' commentary. Our 6,000–7,500 students each year do not need to worry that every instructor employs different criteria to evaluate papers. Here, we are in agreement with Graff that the traditional isolationism of undergraduate courses undermines undergraduate education ("Why Assessment?"). By using a tool such as My Reviewers at a state university, all 30,000 students can be introduced to core academic values, such as the importance of putting sources in dialogue with one another or citing quotations accurately.

By providing an archive of teachers' and peers' comments, a tool such as My Reviewers creates a powerful learning environment. Imagine the benefit of such an archive covering high school through graduate school! Beyond the advantages for students, a tool such as My Reviewers transforms assessment. Universities can adjust their courses in real time to better meet student needs. Rather than impotently wringing their hands in response to problems with undergraduate education identified by studies such as Arum and Roksa's *Academically Adrift,* we can leverage tools such as My Reviewers to track longitudinally the development of students' writing, research, and critical thinking abilities. By creating a culture of assessment, we can tackle the challenges of education in the twenty-first century.

## NOTES

1. This iterative process continues today. In fact, as a process-based community, we continue to revise our evaluative criteria and the development of our pedagogical supportive materials (see http://fyc.usf.edu). Our current rubric is quite different from the one we used in 2008.

2. We realize now, too late, that we neglected to interview instructors involved more actively in the development of My Reviewers, yet some of these contributions are mentioned in Chapters 4 and 5, which mostly address our effort to peer-produce our curriculum.

3. Just as the interface of the online rubric continues to evolve, the criteria undergo constant development and change.

**4**

## Managing a Self-Sustaining Network

*In what ways do our shared pedagogy and online website facilitate instructor collaboration or suggest agency? How do volunteer contributions differ from administratively requested ones? Do instructors who do not contribute to our program through peer-production tools benefit from our online crowdsourcing?*

IN AN INTERVIEW, AUDREY TILTS her chair back on its hind legs and admits that last semester she "wasn't thrilled" with the project options for ENC 1101. So this semester, spring 2009, she decided to pilot two new projects. A first-year master's student in Restoration British literature and a second-semester instructor, Audrey has proven to be a diligent scholar and an inspiring instructor. She spreads her fingers and violently moves her hands to convey *how* much she "really, really liked piloting the projects." She begins to ramble excitedly about which visual artists she favors when teaching her new Taboo project in ENC 1101—Diane Arbus's *Identical Twins* or Pablo Picasso's *Guernica*. Audrey uses art to help students analyze because she believes "we live in an increasingly visual world." She wants students to "flex" their "visual analysis muscles every once in a while, so that they can know when we're being appealed to through a visual argument."

"You know," she continues, "I just want them to make their own visual arguments, because words and images are more alike than they think." And without a breath, she hurriedly adds, "I want, I guess I want, to push them. In the project, they have to critique the effectiveness of the image—like how good it is at making its claim." She ends with, "Oh, and I remind them over and over again that while their opinion is important, they need to stick to the effectiveness of each of the image's elements. Like the regular old rhetorical analysis project." At the end of her talk, when she leans closer to the table, Audrey whispers that "students loved" the project. Recent student evaluations reflect that claim. Dressed in a yellow and white speckled sundress, with rose fabric clips holding back wisps of her curly reddish-brown hair, Audrey seems to revel in this chance to be innovative. She says, "Even when I first started the program, I wanted to come in, be innovative, try new things, fun things, and with the Taboo project I feel like I was able to do that."

This chance to be innovative happens every fall, when graduate student instructors complete their final assignment in the required composition teaching practicum. That project asks students to "work in a group to develop a writing project for the 1101 or 1102 curriculum or program publication (the newsletter, textbook, etc)." In groups of four or five, Joe Moxley asks students to create completely new writing projects, revise ambiguous language in older projects, or create supplemental teaching materials for students. The only initial requirement is that the assignment meet the learning objectives for the writing project it is meant to replace. The projects then undergo a series of peer review sessions well after the practicum is over, and a few might make their way into the curriculum in the spring or the following fall. This project is the first major contribution that graduate student assistants make to the writing program—and in many cases, the last—and its primary goal is to engage graduate students, to make them part of the program's curricular development.

The teaching assistants, many of them beginning teachers like Audrey, are often motivated to perform far beyond the assignment's requirements, bringing with them innovative and creative energy. For instance, Audrey and another of her colleagues, Judy, piloted two new projects each in the second semester at RU. In addition to piloting these projects, Audrey and Judy cowrote an additional project with another two of their peers that had nothing to do with the practicum. This departure from our sponsored projects—many of which are replete with lesson plans and therefore the easiest to teach—indicates that they are intrepid spirits. The FYC staff knew about Audrey's excitement when she created the project in the practicum, but we were unaware that she had actually piloted it. Piloting projects without explicit permission suggests that Audrey felt comfortable enough to assume control of the curriculum. It also suggests that beyond administrative awareness, instructors are effectively contributing to the program. But her individually effective contribution was not uploaded to our official FYC website, even though every instructor in the program has a login and at least some practice using it. That her project remained offline meant that only a small number of her close colleagues knew about Audrey's experimentation, which prevented it and other similar contributions from spreading throughout the faculty and changing the curriculum.

In April 2009, WPAs sent out an email on the FYC listserv asking new instructors which new projects they would prefer to have included in the new curriculum. In her response email, Audrey reflected on her experiences teaching her group's collaborative Taboo project. She cites the project as "actually working quite well": "Students have been engaged discussing what relates to taboo and we've done a lot of activities working toward that." Despite the students' enthusiasm, she forewarns teachers to "set appropriate guidelines and parameters for students." For instance, she "ruled out abortion papers, but others might have other topics to prohibit." Audrey's response indicates a willingness to creatively contribute to the program but only a partial understanding of the program's philosophy and practices. For instance, her project option incorporated some though not all of the common language from the sponsored project, but it is clearly meant to meet the outcomes of that particular project. Paradoxically, it is the project's outcomes that are conspicuously missing from her project description.

When Audrey shared on our listserv her experiences in piloting this project option, she had her colleagues in mind: her email demonstrates her attempt to meaningfully contribute to the core curriculum her peers will use. When she advises that the project still needs "some tweaking," she demonstrates the sense of collaboration and process that we hope to encourage among our teachers. In an attempt to connect the students' exploration of the taboo to critical thinking, she writes, "the creative process would still require a thorough understanding of the elements of rhetorical analysis and provide ample information for writing their papers." Audrey even makes a nod to our program's lack of major creative writing projects: "There has been some concern that incorporating the taboo is inappropriate for a composition classroom; that it does not prepare students for academic writing. . . . But if making students better writers is the goal, we can make them better at one style while having them analyze something other than an article." Notice the push and pull in Audrey's writing: even on this somewhat informal forum, she feels the need to reconcile administrative views with her own. Audrey is departing from the sponsored projects in this instance, but she's taking the road map—the program's learning objectives and outcomes—with her. She's doing so without explicit permission since the project was never submitted to the policy committee, but she teaches with her colleagues in mind, and her email demonstrates an attempt to meaningfully and significantly contribute to the core curriculum that scores of her peers will use.

Despite all this, Audrey's mindset seems to have switched at some point. She reflects in an interview that "I was an author of new projects, but I don't think I will always be that way," and "This year I think I'm going to teach the major [sponsored] projects since it's just easier for me . . . to make my life easier." Audrey's need to simplify her life reminds us that most of our instructors are full-time students who don't have the time to fully immerse themselves in our datagogy. But her need also reinforces the fact that if more instructors contributed to our online curriculum, life might be easier for all the rest. Some instructors stop actively contributing new projects when the practicum ends and their final grades are posted. Audrey, on the other hand, might have continued to teach new projects if doing so wasn't so time-consuming, and if the project webpages were more fully populated with lesson plans representing the collective wisdom of our group. In that sense, the success—or lack thereof—of this practicum project is an excellent way to begin asking the questions of this chapter: What roles do people self-assign within our writing program, and why? How do those roles change, and how do they impinge on our efforts to create agency in the age of peer production?

## IDENTIFYING GOALS AND NETWORKS

Our main goal in this chapter is to reflect on the contact zone between those who contribute to our shared pedagogy and the websites that facilitate their collaboration. Like so many researchers, we arrived here through an evolving set of goals. We began our research for this chapter trying to understand what animates our "gift culture" by positing roles expanded from the work of social scientist Everett M. Rogers, who introduced a paradigm for understanding technological adaptation in his 1962 seminal work *Diffusion of Innovations*. Rogers divided users into five categories, describing how they responded to technological innovation: innovators, early adopters, early majority, late majority, and laggards. After initially asking instructors to identify with one of Rogers's roles, we decided to expand his five original categories into eleven roles that our instructors could more closely identify with, since it quickly became clear that we were examining more than simply acceptance of technological innovation (and because some instructors might not want to label themselves *laggards*). Our expanded list needed to include not only technological contributions, but curricular and interpersonal ones as well. The list included technological identifiers such as "explorer"—someone who "researches and experiments with technologies other than those we host on our servers"—and "downloader"—someone who "points students to the FYC websites via links in Blackboard." Our expanded terminology also included identifiers that focus more on curricular than technological innovation. There were "mentors" and "facilitators," those who "act as guides to incoming teachers" and those who "contribute ideas to the program website," respectively. There were "authors" of new curricular projects, "editors" of existing projects, and "critics," who "provide meaningful critiques that shape the program." We expanded on Rogers's roles to spur productive conversation about program contribution and to investigate why instructors adopted or rejected various technological program tools. We wanted to know how teachers could rethink our writing projects, our teaching objectives, and the way we convey those values.

When we asked our instructors to self-identify as one or more of our new roles, we increasingly became fascinated with this complex web of ways to contribute to the program—from sometimes relying entirely on our program's websites to sometimes completely ignoring them. Someone might be a laggard technologically but a curricular innovator, or she might love technology but hesitate to suggest changes. Because these identifiers can indicate different academic roles, we decided to reconceptualize how we would organize our results to better account for this variety of variables. While there is no way to account for everything, we have selected three especially suggestive characteristics that help us understand how people contribute to our program and how much. These characteristics are *academic status* (e.g., first-year master's student, experienced adjunct, incoming doctoral student, etc.), *pedagogical philosophy* (how the role of the teacher and the writing program are viewed), and *technological adaption* (Rogers's roles relating to technological diffusion). The divisions are not meant to create a taxonomy of possible roles, nor to suggest any sort of formula for how people interact. Rather, they are meant to suggest some of the ways these three characteristics influence an individual's contributions to our program. For instance, our first set of profiles, "The Young and the Restless," examines the responses to our program's collaborative movement by first-year MA students. These teachers share an academic status but differ on their pedagogies and adaption to technology. Moreover, individuals in each of the three major profile sets shared their own subcommunity, so they were able to comment on their influences on one another. Though we could not create a set of profiles for every experience an instructor might have in our program, we tried to select teachers who represented as wide a range as possible. In this chapter, we describe a set of twelve profiles and a larger summation of approximately forty of our eighty instructors.

Tracing our program's online ecology encouraged us to consider how instructors contributed to our program outside of administrative structures or suggestions. We needed to trace the professional experience of our teachers and the interpersonal networks they created amongst themselves outside of the practicum, the mentoring program, or the orientation. In other words, we wanted to find out what motivates instructors to contribute to our program's curriculum, and why instructors such as Audrey would hesitate to consider themselves authors even after writing new prompts. Audrey's example is thought provoking because she pulled away from administrative protocol when she decided to pilot a project, but the results were positive nonetheless.

Therefore, this chapter focuses on the centrifugal forces within our program—but centrifugal force is always compelled by a motion from the center. For instance, if we put water in a bucket and swirl the bucket around on a rope, the water will push away from the center, showing a centrifugal force. Yet that centrifugal force wouldn't show up at all if the bucket weren't spun in the first place. Similarly, the creative, untamed centrifugal forces of our teachers are in some ways prompted in the first place by our program, or by the practicum, the mentoring program, or the larger university. The next chapter, with its focus on how our instructors contribute within a structured mentoring program, can be seen as a mirror image of this chapter, which concentrates on contributions made outside of institutional structures. Both chapters focus on our instructors, but here we explore their use of institutionally influenced technologies to volunteer program contributions. The focus on volunteer contributions made us also consider why so much is contributed by so few—why our program resembles the 80–20 rule, whereby the majority of the contributions are made by a small number of instructors.

Throughout our research, we consider how FYC program staff can share authority in order to balance the tension between the twin needs for teacher autonomy and standardization. We have worked to crowdsource the composition curriculum by enlisting every graduate student, adjunct, and visiting instructor to do a little bit of the work and thus make everyone's life easier. The ideal online marketplace has each merchant bringing his or her wares to the street: one instructor may bring a method for teaching peer review, another one an online resource, and a third a new writing project prompt. Ideally, instructors exchange ideas for ideas in this marketplace. And even though our ideal marketplace is still administratively framed—WPAs set up the website hierarchy and frame online academic conversations around institutional concerns—this marketplace does not have cameras pitched atop lampposts. With a less intrusive administration, this marketplace is an ideal gift culture. Some shop and others sell, but needs are meet through an ongoing exchange of information.

### STORIES FROM THE NETWORK

*The Young and the Restless (Tony, Judy, Claudette, and Audrey)*
Many of our incoming instructors defined themselves with competing but not quite contradictory roles. They were experimenters, trying new projects, innovative lesson plans, or new types of technology. But they also defined themselves as novices who felt unsure that their contributions merited the attention of their peers. Moreover, they understandably felt an intense responsibility to their students. They wanted to try new projects, but they also felt that trying new pedagogical approaches could wait while they became more experienced teachers. Having never taught before, many made little distinction between more traditional teaching practices and our program's heavy reliance on technology: it was all new to them. The four teachers profiled in this section all interact with one another in person and online. They went through the practicum together, teach the same courses, and share an office together. These four MA students—among others—form a tightly knit subcommunity that shares an office, graduate classes, a similar teaching schedule, and similar degree plans.

Tony sees himself as a technology mentor to the group but far less experimental in his own teaching. Whenever instructors have a technological issue, they come to him because he's very comfortable working with SharePoint and Blackboard. It's not so much that he has the answers, but having worked with technology in his previous jobs as a technical writer, he knows where to find information and has the motivation to do so. There's no fear in Tony's voice when speaking about technology, but there isn't necessarily love either. Though he certainly feels at home with technology, he doesn't consider himself an innovator. In his teaching or in his personal life, he's "willing to try to use just about anything" but doesn't "really consider [himself] trying anything new." In fact, he defines his and his peers' academic roles in contextual terms rather than according to internal predisposition. For instance, when asked to define the roles of his peers, he says, "I would say we're all innovators or early adopters; I guess you have to be because we're all new," and he later notes, "I don't see myself growing or evolving until something changes; I've become very comfortable with how I do things with teaching and technology, and won't change until I need to." There is no hint or tone of resistance, simply a desire to maintain the status quo, at least for now.

Part of that desire to maintain the status quo comes from Tony's inexperience in the classroom. Though fearless using unfamiliar technologies, he has far less experience addressing and solving pedagogical problems. As a result, he's willing to push himself down the scale of innovation:

> I do use wikis for some for my teaching. I'm definitely more of an early adopter in most of my life, but I would identify myself as an early adopter or early majority with my teaching. There's just more responsibility. It [teaching] matters more; I don't want to screw something up. There's people staring at me; people evaluating me; I don't want to mess their lives up.

Maintaining the status quo is a way of guaranteeing quality control during teaching. Tony admits that, since the practicum, he has not added more content, such as lesson plans or links, to the program website. It's not so much a matter of time as it is motivation. He suspects that few of his colleagues will visit the site to see what he has uploaded and that leaves him wondering if uploading the material is worth the trouble: "The problem is, well, it's like double the work, and since nobody does it, it becomes futile. It's basically a self-fulfilling prophecy after a while of not using it." Consequently, he gravitates most toward the role of editor, someone who takes preexisting content and adapts it—"tweaks" as he puts it—for a particular classroom's purpose.

When Tony tweaks content already on our FYC site, he performs the collaborative equivalent of what Clay Shirky terms *sharing*. Sharing is the simplest type of collaboration because such websites "operate in a largely take-it-or-leave-it fashion, which allows for the maximum freedom of the individual to participate while creating the fewest complications of group life" (49). This type of collaboration involves the contribution of lesson plans, readings, links to interesting websites, and worksheets. Most of these contributions can be found on our website's major project pages, which provide a description of the project, its key objectives, and its authors. In the right-hand columns, users will find a variety of document libraries and a links list to useful websites, lesson plans, PowerPoints, videos, and worksheets.

Tony has become less likely to contribute teaching ideas to the program since his participation in the practicum. He understands "the overarching idea is that if everyone put information on these pages then we would be able to share all of our content." Tony knows that if all instructors uploaded to the webpages, everyone's life would be easier. But the majority of instructors do not contribute. According to our data, the site has had more than five million hits in the last year, but only eighteen instructors have added material to the major project webpages. Therefore, Tony sees our ideal marketplace as strictly ideal; it works more in principle than in application. From his perspective, the structure of our website involves a type of self-fulfilling prophecy. When orientation ends, and later when the practicum grades are posted and the mentoring program has ended for the semester, instructors have less incentive to contribute online, especially if there's no guarantee that others will appreciate their work. With each instructor aware that his or her colleagues have fewer incentives to contribute online, the social contract of contributing to a datagogy is broken. This reasoning is the logic of the 80–20 rule from someone who is part of the 80 percent.

Though we discuss the 80–20 rule in depth in Chapter 1, a brief refresher is worthwhile here. Clay Shirky reminds us that a small group of contributors (perhaps few as two or three) can account for the vast majority of the work in a complex system of contributions (124–28). Shirky notes, for instance, that "[t]he Wikipedia article on asphalt has 129 contributors making 205 total edits, but the bulk of the work was contributed by a small fraction of participants, and just six accounted for about a quarter of the edits" (123). He makes two interesting observations about the wide variance in contributions. First, he observes that "the imbalance is the same shape across a huge number of different kinds of behaviors" and, second, that "the imbalance drives large social systems rather than damaging them" (125). Both of Shirky's observations—if we are to accept them—act like an editor offering bittersweet advice to our program's datagogical narrative. The advice is sweet because Shirky's praise of the 80–20 rule implies that our struggles to encourage instructors to contribute are reminiscent of the dynamics at highly successful websites such as Wikipedia and Flickr. We can see from our own statistical data that our contribution pattern bears an uncanny resemblance to this widely pronounced phenomenon, and formal interviews and hallway conversations demonstrate that a relatively small number of significant contributors is still "enough to create profound value for millions of users" (125). Despite these consolations, our program's similarities to so many other complex systems imply that there is a sort of glass ceiling on sharing that has not been broken, and which might not even be practical or even desirable to break.

Even though Tony doesn't upload material to our FYC site, he still uses "the project pages that are nicely set up because they have so much of what you need." He drew from the site heavily his first semester, occasionally added to it, and even pointed students there. Offline he listens and occasionally shares ideas with his office mates about what works in the classroom, though even there he identifies himself as less likely than others to collaborate. His use of these projects pages demonstrates some movement toward a shared curriculum and some success at community, but it also underscores the fact that our online community is not nearly as interactive as it could be. This is a consequence of what Tony sees as a lack of excitement among instructors, coupled with a lack of organizational sophistication within the site. For instance, when he points his students directly to the project pages, he can't guarantee the quality or relevance of what they will find: "students go on to them and grab random things and do really weird stuff. . . . It's frustrating to them and to me because I can't really say, 'It's your fault. I gave you the link, and instructors just wrote some really weird stuff.'" This confusion among students underscores the need to rethink whether an online community for instructors can simultaneously be an online community for students.

Judy and Claudette also both identify themselves as early adopters, and they are comfortable but not as confident with technology as Tony. Like Tony, Judy and Claudette do not have previous college-level teaching experience, but Claudette does have a few years of experience teaching middle school. Their respective teaching experience turned out to be one of the most significant reasons why each did or didn't try new technologies, create new projects, or share their self-authored lesson plans. Claudette, who has the most teaching experience, clearly generates the most original content; each of her closest colleagues identifies her as the most likely to share information with each of them privately and then to upload it later to our FYC site. When she reflects on her experiences sharing material online, Claudette's words reveal how her pedagogical approach has been informed by her experience: "I started uploading the first semester; it was a really great place for everybody to share their ideas. I've always been of a mindset as a teacher, just always sharing, and I'm glad to see that there is a place to do that online." Though her colleagues don't speculate as to why she is the most active collaborator, Claudette does, assuming that it has something to do with her years of teaching middle school before coming to graduate school. The connection she sees between experience and collaborative efforts helps explain Tony's fear that if he pushes the boundaries technologically or pedagogically he may "screw up" his students' educations. The same relationship between experience

and contributions explains why Judy believes that "the biggest ob-
stacle to becoming authors is that we don't have the experience or
confidence to create something, but we're smart enough to follow
a guide or revise it after receiving it." In our interviews with each
of these three instructors, they emphasized the website as a "guide"
to innovate from. As Claudette explains, "Before each project, I go
through those pages to see what other people are doing, and then
I see how I can use that to present the project." She uses only the
main website and avoids the less popular experimental sites and
her own personal "My Site" (a SharePoint Web space for each instructor to create a professional profile). Instead, Claudette focuses
on the "project pages" that function as a repository of information
where instructors can give and find ideas. Claudette echoes the attitude of many of our instructors with her enthusiasm for these
pages: "I love the project pages because you get an idea of what
other people are doing!"

Judy's lack of confidence affects everything she does in terms
of contributing online and onsite. When she first entered the program, she feared that her contributions would not be significant or
important enough. If she came up with an innovative lesson plan
that primarily related to what she and her office mates—Claudette
and Tony—were doing, she would consider it "irrelevant" and "too
specific" for the general instructor population. She describes indis-
criminately uploading during her first semester just "whatever" she
had created for her class, but now she uploads fewer items that are
more strategically considered: "I guess I upload more significant
stuff now than in the past, but that probably has more to do with
my experience as a teacher, but I just don't upload as much anymore." Ironically, it's Judy's frequent use of the shared resources
on the project pages that makes her most hesitant to upload something. Her reliance on these resources means that much of the material she authors is really just a variation of something someone
else has already created, and she does not want to "tread" on what
anyone else has done.

Part of this reluctance to "tread" speaks to two larger problems
with our online collaboration efforts—a shared sense of online

folkways and adequate training. Judy expanded on her fears of treading by explaining that "you can share something, but you just throw something up there, and it just sits there in the pile of stuff. People upload things but don't really show how or why they used it. I wish there was a way to comment on an uploaded link or file." The problem here is an overabundance of information without adequate annotation. The more information added to a project page, the more difficult it is to find any one particular source because little of it is commented on. The simple steps needed to find and share information on these pages are their greatest asset, but that simplicity prevents a sophisticated organization of the material. Adding to these pages is fairly simple, and almost everyone in our program—from the innovators to the laggards—knows in principle how to use this aspect of our site. Adding pages only requires pasting a URL or uploading a file—similar to an attachment in email and taking only a few moments. Unfortunately, SharePoint 2007 doesn't allow uploaded material to be easily reorganized according to relevance, popularity, or subject matter (methods of reorganizing materials are too complex for most users). On SharePoint's links lists and document libraries, the order of material depends mostly on when it was uploaded, so the earliest shared documents receive the most attention from site visitors. Since the document libraries on our project pages are linked from other pages, many novice contributors do not easily see how to annotate their contributions (as in Figure 4.1).

If users follow the document library links to the document library main page, an ambiguous-looking icon appears, from which contributors can annotate their work. But many do not take this step, which means that the content of many contributions is clear only once the file has been clicked on—hardly the most efficient model. When we first began our website, these limitations mattered much less because of the paucity of material that needed to be organized. But with each new semester, another generation of graduate students and adjuncts shares material, slowing the pace of accessing our accumulated resources and suggesting that we have reached a tipping point, where more information is not necessarily better without a reconsideration of how we organize and privilege it.

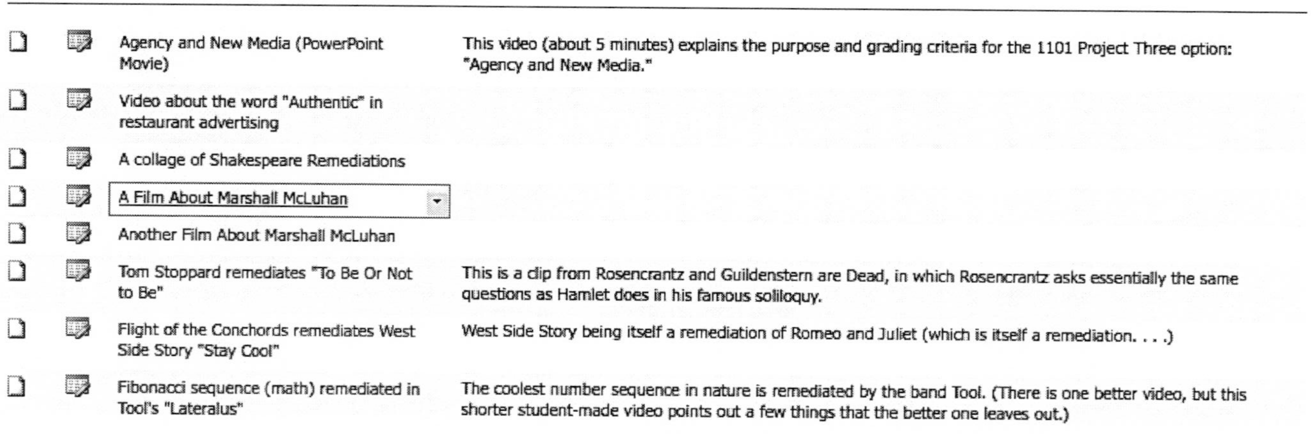

☐ 📄 Agency and New Media (PowerPoint Movie)
This video (about 5 minutes) explains the purpose and grading criteria for the 1101 Project Three option: "Agency and New Media."

☐ 📄 Video about the word "Authentic" in restaurant advertising

☐ 📄 A collage of Shakespeare Remediations

☐ 📄 A Film About Marshall McLuhan ▶

☐ 📄 Another Film About Marshall McLuhan

☐ 📄 Tom Stoppard remediates "To Be Or Not to Be"
This is a clip from Rosencrantz and Guildenstern are Dead, in which Rosencrantz asks essentially the same questions as Hamlet does in his famous soliloquy.

☐ 📄 Flight of the Conchords remediates West Side Story "Stay Cool"
West Side Story being itself a remediation of Romeo and Juliet (which is itself a remediation. . . .)

☐ 📄 Fibonacci sequence (math) remediated in Tool's "Lateralus"
The coolest number sequence in nature is remediated by the band Tool. (There is one better video, but this shorter student-made video points out a few things that the better one leaves out.)

Figure 4.1. A selection of contributions to our FYC site, some with comments or annotations

When we combine the fact that uploaded documents or links are organized chronologically in the order they were shared with the lack of annotations on uploaded material, the problem Judy spoke of becomes apparent. Judy understands the datagogical ethos, but she also understands the unintended consequences of putting up too much information. As a result, she still uploads material, she reports, but she's more careful to upload only what she finds especially helpful or truly original. Her wariness echoes Tony's fear that students will find something "random" online that will mess them up.

Equally important is the question of training; Judy's concern about labeling content is actually something SharePoint does quite well, and after our interview with her, we introduced her to the commenting function for uploaded material. But that she was unaware of this function underscores Claudette's observation that instructors feel all of these strategies and ways of collaborating are "overwhelming." We need to work more on scaffolding our technological training. These hesitancies to contribute pose a problem because only part of our goal is to create a shared pedagogy; an equally significant part is to do so through "the wisdom of the crowds" and through the professionalization of instructors, which we hope will happen in part through a network of sharing. But what happens if most of that sharing is unevenly distributed?

One constructive response to this dilemma—and the one we have taken—is to try to reimagine what "shared pedagogy" means, to redefine how collaboration happens, and to think of our pedagogical marketplace as having an "underlife," which works in subtle concert with our administratively sponsored websites. Robert Brooke, writing about underlife in the composition classroom, states that "in contemporary writing instruction, both students and teachers undercut the traditional roles of the American educational system in order to substitute more complex identities in their place" (141). If we apply Brooke's understanding of classroom "underlife" to our instructors' methods of sharing, a new picture begins to emerge. These master's students have a network, a subcommunity through which they share pedagogical ideas. Judy and

Claudette constantly communicate with each other about lesson plans and teaching ideas, and they contribute some PowerPoints, YouTube links, and helpful websites to our Web Part Pages, even after completing the practicum. Judy observes, after her critique of the uploading feature, that she's "actually impressed with how much of a community we have." But both are quick to point out that they don't upload most of what they create or revise—which isn't to say they don't share it with the program at large; they just don't do so in a way that is obvious to WPAs. They reported feeling "overwhelmed" during orientation or just too busy to share ideas, with classes, teaching, and publishing quickly becoming much more pressing concerns. Claudette proposed waiting until the end of the semester and then having an upload party: "I wonder if there is a way of reminding people at the end of the semester when things have slowed down, when they're less busy and more likely to upload things." However, she probably didn't know that an upload party had been held at the end of the semester before she arrived—but only one non–staff teacher attended.

Enter Audrey, who you are already familiar with. She has a decidedly different relationship with technology from that of her peers. Audrey is active in our graduate organization and in the mentoring program. Her participation in these programs results partly from her self-definition as a "social" person. She describes herself as a laggard or late majority in every aspect of her life: "my phone doesn't even have a camera." From her perspective, using technology is all part of a zero-sum game in which schoolwork, her "life" outside of school, her teaching, and her professional development all compete for time. The more time she devotes to technology, the less she has for everything else. Nothing better epitomizes this attitude than her relationship with email: "I hate it! I have this relationship to my email box, so when my email box is empty, my life is organized. And when I get these emails with all these things that I can or should be doing, I just get overwhelmed, and I delete them." However, Audrey also states her intense desire to be an innovator by piloting two new projects created by her peers and sharing her teaching advice with incoming students. It would be unfair to say she's resistant to using technology, but she doesn't see it as central to her professional identity. Her aversion to technology explains why she didn't properly upload her Taboo project proposal so that her peers could view it and add suggestions through the Web Part option. When she uses the major project pages, she finds them "very helpful," and she was glad to learn during orientation how to contribute to them. Much of Audrey's aversion comes from technology that seems like unsolicited background noise: "The listserv stuff, I just hate getting so many emails that say 'Oh, try this, try this, try this'; if it's important, just put it on the instructor page." And Blackboard, institutionally required, causes Audrey an equal amount of angst: "My biggest frustration was Blackboard. We got used to one version and just as I became comfortable with it, RU changed it. I hate the new Blackboard; I hate it! The fyc.usf.edu website is helpful and intuitive for the most part. I like it for project ideas, but I don't use it for anything else. I find all of that really good." Audrey, then, much like her MA peers, is part of the shared pedagogical community, but the emphasis of her online involvement is more on what she uses than what she contributes. Offline, in her shared subcommunity with Tony, Judy, and Claudette, she is creating new projects, sharing them, and coordinating lesson plans.

### The Bold and the Beautiful (Marlene and Henry)

When it comes to using technology, there is no one bolder than Marlene, who at the time of her interview had just completed her first year of adjunct teaching. To understand her academic role, we need to examine both her online and her onsite presence. Like Claudette, Marlene had previous teaching experience but spent much of it in grades K–12, and therefore she came to college teaching with some trepidation. However, she looked on her struggles as problems that needed solutions—which is, as it happens, the same perspective she has on technology. Marlene describes her identity entering the program as a "downloader and an advocate," but she's eager to change that. She explains, "I'm striving to become an author, and an explorer; that's the direction that I'm heading in; and a collaborator; that's where I'm going; I'm not there yet." What compounded her trepidation was the suddenness of her hiring, just days before the semester started. She describes our FYC site and more generally the FYC program as incredibly complex: "Just understanding the system at the beginning; it's unavoidable to feel a little overwhelmed; there's so much to learn. So it's just a matter of learning how to participate. I've been out of the university setting for a lot of years, so I want to make sure my contribution is valuable."

Though Marlene was overwhelmed at first, she constantly sought out help from the program's mentors and coordinators. (Because she was an adjunct, she wasn't assigned a mentor.) Living far from campus with office hours different from those of her adjunct office mates made it even harder for her to feel connected. Nevertheless, Marlene had no problem searching out help, always asking questions or just coming in to the mentoring office to chat: "I really value a work environment where you can walk down the hall and talk." Acutely aware of the position she was in and how it differed from those of the mentors, she worked to be more engaged, both online and onsite. Her relationship to technology can be described as fearless and goal driven:

> I see myself as between the innovator and the early adopter because I'm looking for solutions, and when I come up with something that I want to work better, I look to see what's out there, do reviews, see what people are saying . . . sometimes, most of the time . . . and if looks like it might work, I'll try it. But sometimes, if I'm in a desperate situation or if what I'm looking for a solution to is not critical, then I'll just try something new that's out there.

In stark contrast to Audrey, Marlene sees technology as central to her teaching and to her life. Whereas Audrey was overwhelmed by too many emails, Marlene finds comfort in technology and how it can streamline her life. She transfers this enthusiasm to her teaching as well. She creates videos for her students and models them after PowerPoint videos created by collaborators. She's thinking about uploading to YouTube and creating movie trailers—because her instructional videos are too large to upload to our site or attach to emails. During an interview, she explains, "I love to just sit in my office and to develop stuff." But when Marlene discusses developing materials, it's always in conjunction with what someone else is doing, feeding off the ideas of others and their responses. In this vein, she attends an annual set of seminars on instructional technology hosted by another campus department, even though attendance isn't required. When reflecting on what she's learned, she recalls logging in more than twenty-seven hours and only regretting that more people in our department don't take advantage of the available lessons and networking.

Over the last year, Marlene's ability to use our main FYC site has gone from novice to adept, but she still feels some frustration at its unnecessary complexity. This frustration arose as she was trying to upload content. Much like the younger instructors, Marlene buys into our datagogical concept but finds impediments to sharing. The obstacles don't seem to faze her, however; they are simply problems that require solutions. In fact, she describes in glowing terms our online networks, calling them "genius" and "revolutionary" despite their need for improvement. The site is, in her words, a "perfect blend of structure and autonomy." After twelve months in our program, Marlene describes herself as "ready to rock 'n roll," and she has actively engaged in revising our curriculum by attending administrative and curricular meetings. She describes herself as much more confident in the program now and is even considering commuting on days when she isn't teaching just to be physically closer to the program so that she can be more attuned to the day-to-day conversations between mentors, administrators, and her fellow instructors. She sees this proximity as critical to being involved in the program's curricular development; she emphasizes how much of the collaborative culture of our program exists not just online or in official meetings, but also in the daily minutiae and small conversations that happen in the hallways and offices. Like Audrey, Marlene searches for professional social engagement, albeit in a different sphere. Marlene's goal is to synchronize the technologies she uses:

Obviously, once you've found a solution, then it kind of seeps into your life. So my latest thing right now is to get totally synchronized with everything. So I just got my new Mac-Book, I've got my new iTouch [iPod Touch]; I got the iTouch because I don't want the forced data plan with the iPhone. But then I found that I can also link my regular cell phone, and then with the MobileMe I can sync to my PC and *I. Am. Just. So. Thrilled.* I found the little iTouch app where I can store my passwords, and then my Gmail can link into my university email, so everything is coming together. This summer is the summer of synchronization.

As an adjunct, Marlene doesn't have a strictly defined face-to-face community with which to share; she also didn't have a mentor or the ability to participate in the practicum, and due to timing, her office is often quiet. And yet Marlene manages to develop material and contribute to the program, doing the "double" work Tony wishes more instructors would engage in.

Before teaching in our writing program, Henry had never been a college instructor, but he has had an accomplished professional life, working in a variety of fields, always with significant responsibility. He is no stranger to public speaking and he has taught, but not in a traditional classroom. Henry had a way with words when we interviewed him; he encapsulated in a memorable way the ideas other instructors expressed indirectly. This verbal precision may stem in part from his previous management experience or from his observations of how others in his previous career interacted with technology. Whatever the source, this precision and the breadth of his empathy make him stand out: he empathized with those who had experiences different from his own, and he articulated their concerns with uncanny precision.

Two of Henry's observations are especially intriguing: *the fire hose effect*[1] and the *u-curve*. He describes the fire hose effect as "providing too much complexity too soon when introducing a new technology." He then elaborates on this point: "When I first got here, technological tools were too populous; they were unnecessarily overwhelming. I wanted a drink of water and someone turned

the fire hose on. I asked what time it was and you built me a clock."
Entering the program with much younger peers like Judy, Henry
has the same hesitancy about embracing technology. He identifies
himself as an early adopter in most of his life but as a member
of the early majority in his teaching because of his "hesitations in
other areas of the programs." Much like Tony, Henry is less likely
to boldly experiment since it's all new. In addition, what separates
him from the innovators is that he wants a little guidance on how a
tool can be used: "I like to be given a script and then improvise off
that script; when I'm introduced to a new tool, I need to be shown
how to use it. I'm not going to be the first to figure out how to use
it. So I need someone to tell me, 'Here's what the program is; here
is how you can best use it.' [I need s]ome base practice."

Beyond expressing how we can better introduce tools to instructors, Henry articulates the extremes he has noticed within our
program's subcommunities, what we might call the "the u-curve":
"The people I've encountered so far in the program; I would say
that they fall into either extreme; they tend to either be innovators
or early adopters, or late majority and laggards. I don't really see a
bell curve there." What Henry went on to describe sounded like
an inverted bell curve, a *u-curve*, although he didn't use that term
himself. Here, Henry explains our 80–20 distribution and identifies a few reasons why that u-curve might occur. He identifies the
faculty, mentors, and facilitators as those who see "technology as
an important portal for how we communicate" and who are "willing to embrace new ideas and new technology into the program."
On the other "extreme," his office mates and other instructors are
"very hesitant" to use the FYC websites, online rubric, and even
Blackboard. The reasons vary, from lack of confidence about how
to use the tools, to antipathy toward technology, to an opinion
that "we're here to teach literature and not technology." In his own
work, Henry actually defies the u-curve paradigm, for he repeatedly
defines himself as someone who is a "mosaic" of identities: author,
editor (especially), advocate (on the listserv, in the halls, and in the
offices), critic, technician (when he can be), mentor (increasingly
so), and collaborator (in a limited sense). He is skeptical about

some of the ways the technology is employed, but rejects any term like *disconnected, downloader,* or *tourist* that would indicate technology has pushed him out of the community. As already mentioned, he identifies himself as an early adopter when using technology but "bumps" that down to early majority when working within the FYC program. When asked why, he didn't miss a beat before offering a hypothesis, though he admits he hadn't ever thought of the shift before in that way:

> I think possibly because of hesitations in the other areas of the program: coming as a new graduate student, as a new teacher, in a new environment, with new faces, both a personal, interpersonal, and a professional and academic method—I think that those just all create kind of cautions and barriers that mean I'm going to be a little more critical about each of the choices I make, both how they affect me personally, as well as most specifically how they affect my ability to perform in front of a classroom or among my peers.

But Henry's hesitation wasn't permanent. During his first year, he avoided being a "mentor" or especially an "explorer," but by his second year he began to feel confident about his mastery of the program and the technology. He became an official mentor to new graduate students in our program in his third semester. The hesitancy he expressed early on has overtones of Tony's and Judy's wariness about branching out too much too early, but his previous professional experience made him feel no hesitancy in speaking up about concerns and questions. That experience eventually gave him the same confidence that Marlene and Claudette expressed: he can even see the "potential long-term" possibility of becoming an explorer, and he feels very strongly about our program's listserv as a way to find multiple answers to simple questions because that tool offers a way of creating community in an "environment" that otherwise at times feels "isolated."

Henry's observations are notable for several reasons. As an advocate for the listserv, he reminds us how many of our instructors speak highly of the simple structure of the project pages, in contrast to their and his skepticism of the myriad more complex tools we offer. More to the point, Henry critiques the way we introduce those tools as self-defeating: too much, too fast. There is increasing evidence that the fire hose effect is contributing to the u-curve, yet Henry's own "mosaic" identity demonstrates that instructors have more complex identities and progressions than appearances may indicate. The u-curve (or 80–20 rule) conceals the professional growth of "The Young and the Restless" and "The Bold and the Beautiful," just as it concealed Henry's own progression. Of course, neither of these groups really illuminates the perspective of instructors who are intimidated by or feel antipathy for all things technological. Their story needs to be told too.

*Guiding Light (Lauren, Vivian, and Shirley)*

No depiction of our program's propensity to use technology would be complete without a review of instructors who fit Everett Rogers's descriptions of late adopters and laggards. The instructors who need a guiding light to help them understand how to use our technology do not see our websites and wikis as helpful tools to supplement their teaching preparations, nor do they view online social networking as an opportunity to share ideas with their peers. Just as important, from their perspective these tools are not a philosophical pillar of an overarching programmatic philosophy—i.e., a way to tap into the "the wisdom of the crowds." Instead, technology is an impediment to getting the job done. Recall Audrey's aversion to technologies, even those required by the university: "I hate the new Blackboard; I hate it!" Whenever Audrey has problems with technology, she says, she just complains until somebody, anybody, fixes it.

This sense of an overwhelming influx of information and possibilities was shared by other instructors, especially those who identified themselves as late majority or laggards. For instance, Shirley, a doctoral student in literature and an active contributor to our FYC program's curriculum, recounts her early frustration with the prevalence of technology: "I was overwhelmed by the technology aspect. There was a lot of repetition of material and websites. During orientation, there were a lot of people who were trying to click and show and demonstrate on the big screen where these things were, and that made it more confusing." Her negative reference to a "lot of people" undermines our reliance on many mentors and facilitators—rather than just WPAs—to provide assistance to teachers during orientation and throughout the semester. Whereas Marlene found strength in these numerous technological and human resources, Shirley indicates that this leadership model can also splinter the focus of the program. For instance, during the 2007 fall orientation, when Shirley first came to RU, we offered our teachers two major websites—CollegeWriting.us and Eportfolio, the latter providing both a private permissions Web space just for teachers and a public space for instructors and students. We maintained two secondary wiki sites (writingwiki.org and teachingwiki.org), a blogging site (writingblogs.org), and Blackboard, which RU requires that we use to post grades and syllabi. Additionally, Blackboard has its own blogging and wiki functions, though it has no capacity for cross-class conversations or sharing of information among faculty.

The multiplicity of websites probably had a disorienting effect because we didn't clarify which websites were more important—Blackboard or the multiple FYC sites. But the websites alone didn't create the "fire hose effect"; as Shirley put it, there were "a lot of people" presenting new information, each with his or her own brief moment to explain a tool. More often than not, each mentor or facilitator was assigned to lead the discussion of the technology that he or she excelled at using in his or her own class. This method of introducing new material had the benefit of providing expert instruction, but it must have looked different from a newcomer's perspective: everyone with a parochial interest and perhaps no clarity about what was essential. All of these technological options, of course, are competing for time and interest with our assessment efforts, our curriculum, and our overall FYC policies—which is to say, teachers have a lot to learn in two weeks. This resulted in an abrupt shift in perception for Shirley as she began to teach composition: "My impression changed a lot; I initially thought we were very technologically orientated, and I initially thought you had to be a participant in technological advancements in order to be successful in the program. But I don't think that is true anymore. In reality, it's just not that important." From her perspective, the technology can be an asset for those who are so inclined. The problem, she notes, is that so many of our faculty members are on the low-tech side of the digital divide that all of this technology can be divisive. It can exacerbate the U-shaped split that Henry spoke of, and by doing so leave some feeling less empowered. It's like a group of peers inviting a kid to play baseball, forgetting that not everyone has a glove and a mitt—not to mention those who do but don't care for the sport.

Shirley agreed that the goals behind the multiplicity of techno-logical tools were laudable. When asked to define those goals, she responded that they were there to "make the bureaucratic distinc-tions [between administrators and teachers] less mystical" so that everyone can "see what you can do." The tools are designed to cre-ate "a leveling between the powers that be and the teachers." This is a fair if not complete summation of the intent behind our use of technology to increase teacher agency. When asked whether the re-liance on technology fails because of execution or the concept itself, she said, "It's just not the best way of going about it. It's ultimately exclusive." But she later amended, "I would just like to add that those things are very useful; just because I don't use them, doesn't mean other people wouldn't find them very useful."

What *has* had a benevolent influence on her teaching are such things as the mentoring program, the graduate composition practi-cum, and orientation in general. In fact, she speaks very highly of the mentoring program, explaining that it has afforded her the greatest sense of agency and community within the program. She describes herself as a "paper person," preferring to hold text and to talk to people one on one, which she feels fosters a sense of infor-mality. The idea that peer-production technology could facilitate conversation is anathema to Shirley. In her first semester of teach-ing, she often reviewed the website for ideas but came away frus-trated. While the website "could potentially be a tool for commu-nity," she feels that it currently fails to achieve that purpose because "there is no sense of dialogue online." The asynchronous nature of

SharePoint Web Parts keeps her from asking questions about a lesson plan, and that dialogue is what counts for her: "For instance, if I created a lesson plan about how to teach thesis writing that someone else didn't like, we couldn't go back and forth learning a new way." This critique aptly points to the site's emphasis on asynchronous technology at the expense of more immediate communication like instant messaging.

Nevertheless, Shirley doesn't oppose the emphasis on online peer production but instead thinks it needs something to "complement" it, such as a face-to-face program or group. It's important to reconcile this final claim with her earlier statement that peer-production technology excludes people. After all, if the online emphasis is part of a larger ecology, then how can it also be an exclusive environment? Furthermore, how can the program be simultaneously exclusive because of technology and yet—as she observes—*not* be a major factor for "success" in the program? Part of the seeming contradiction may be a matter of emphasis—the online features of our program receive more focus, or at least are perceived to. Part is undoubtedly the chaotic and "fire hose" introduction of technology. But another part probably derives from the fact that the bureaucratic mechanisms for change in our program are all connected to our main website. For instance, Shirley created a project just as the instructors discussed at the beginning of this chapter did, and her project, with some modifications, was integrated into the program. Authors of a new writing project are encouraged to play a role during each stage of that project's implementation, and when asked why she didn't participate in the wider implementation of her own project, Shirley responded, "I don't think I would know how to have my hands in it. I would not know how to go about affecting the way it was revised. But I have had my hands in it through the mentoring program." And later she added a reflection regarding orientation that speaks to this point: "I think partly because I am more of a print person in general. If I had a printout of all the information, something that I could look at instead of seeing it on screen, then it would be better." From Shirley's reflections, we can conclude that while the technology aspect of our program does not prevent someone from thriving, its complexity can exclude instructors from the online community it creates. There exists alongside this community several others, including one created by the mentoring program. While these communities are intermingled, Shirley's testimony clearly indicates that they do not yet seamlessly fit into one larger ecology. To create a sense of agency in the age of peer production, then, more work needs to be done to interweave the practices of these two worlds. Just as Marlene felt somewhat excluded from the mentoring community because of her schedule and lack of contact with other instructors, so Shirley felt indifferent to the online community. As a program, we need to do a better job of redesigning each community to engage those least likely to thrive in it, so that we have one larger community with many smaller subcommunities.

Vivian is another PhD student in our program whose indifference to technology prevents her from becoming an integral part of the program. Vivian is a specialist in rhetoric and composition, and it's clear she has ideas regarding how to improve the curriculum, but unlike Shirley, she keeps most of her ideas to herself. At least she did during her first year in the program. When Vivian first entered our program, she felt a sense of isolation, having moved from a different part of the country. Her reluctance to involve herself might stem partly from the ethos of her previous program, which emphasized keeping ideas to oneself for fear of having them stolen. But another, larger part of Vivian's hesitation is her aversion to anything technologically complicated. It's not that she's a Luddite: "I use technology all the time, just not this website." Her favorite website to reference for its usability is Facebook.

From Vivian's perspective, Facebook is simple and intuitive and does not involve a steep learning curve. Moreover, Facebook doesn't offer a lot of options—at least for beginners, which makes it comforting. Though Facebook users can be creative in posting updates, creating notes, or sharing photos, those basic features don't change, and the architecture of the site remains similar even through interface tweaks. In contrast, every instructor in our program has the option to create links lists, document libraries, and even webpages on the FYC site (though few know how), and they have the opportunity to contribute links and documents to existing pages. Which is to say that whereas Facebook is a closed system, where the input doesn't affect the system itself, our site is an open system, meaning that what people contribute not only adds to the website but also in many cases changes the structure of the site itself—or at least it can. Perhaps because most instructors are familiar with Facebook, they treat our website as if they were active or passive members on Facebook—contributors or lurkers, respectively, to a closed system. The active members, such as Marlene and Claudette, voluntarily contribute material, but they don't affect the look of the page, and their contributions follow the simplest routes. The passive members, such as Audrey and Tony, have no trouble lurking on the site, viewing what others have done, just as lurkers on Facebook view updates without updating themselves. And they never add anything. Vivian represents many instructors who are lurkers despite their reluctance and hesitation. "I use whatever is on the tabs; unless it's on those tabs, I don't use it," she reminds us several times. It's not that she hasn't tried to learn how to use these tools, but there is a tone of fatalism in her voice when she describes trying to translate our technology into her own vernacular: "When we're in groups in orientation or in the practicum, it's hard for me to follow; and if I get one or two steps behind, then I'm done; I'm lost. At some point I think, 'Well, I've already asked three people how to do something.' I don't learn well with the whole class—and if you get behind, you're screwed. Once I'm lost, then I'm lost, and I'm done. I'm better one on one."

Over her first year in the program, Vivian began showing more interest in contributing to the curriculum. When asked if she would like to contribute some new projects and revise old ones, she responded, "Absolutely, I want to do that," but she felt at a loss as to how to get started. Nevertheless, she does see herself making progress in understanding the website and says that "she might evolve further." But much like Shirley, Vivian's reflections demonstrate that the program needs to evolve to make her feel more welcome. What's so disheartening about their reactions is that each *could* submit new ideas to the WPAs in person rather than digitally, have someone upload their material for them, or work with them one on one. But the pressures of graduate school, early miscommunication, and an understandable sense of frustration impede those possibilities.

Another similarity between Vivian and Shirley is that they both reflect on the culture shock they experienced at RU. The distinctions between their old schools and RU are much greater than simply the technological requirements: Shirley explains, "This program is much more rigid in its expectations than my previous school. So it forced me to think through how to meet its goals and my own for teaching. Mentoring has definitely forced me to reflect more on my teaching." The provocation toward self-reflection is a trait they share with Lauren, a very experienced adjunct who has taught several years at RU. She came from a large university that provided opportunities to use technology in the classroom but didn't require its use: "When I came here, I came from a school that offered me the opportunity to teach in an entirely computer generated class; but I didn't do it because I was so scared." That fear of technology carried over to her first encounters with the requirements at RU. She remembers, "When I first came to [RU], they had that little seminar, and I thought, 'God, I'll never get this.' There was one adjunct who knew about computers, but the rest of us all began to teach each other in the office." Lauren describes herself as a paper person and a writer of a different generation, someone who still handwrites eight-page letters to friends. She has never integrated technology into her life as Marlene has; nevertheless, Lauren describes herself as an intrepid spirit who learns something new each semester: "I'm using the overhead projector and blogs [and] I'm just amazed at how much better I've gotten at Blackboard. I never thought I would be able to do that." Whenever she doesn't understand something, she seeks out the answer, asking "anyone who has any knowledge about the technology." From her point of view, Joe Moxley has made her feel "very comfortable" within the program, though she does admit, "If I get into a conversation [with him], I'm just going to get lost."

While Lauren's words definitely do not indicate proficiency with peer-production technology, her drive to understand more basic technological skills has contributed to a productive face-to-face community. And she has transitioned from mentee to mentor because of her relationship with fellow adjuncts: "My office mates come and ask me questions and make me feel like a genius." But Lauren always views technology as a possible—though certainly not inevitable—competitor with her students for her attention; she fears that learning new technologies will distract her from helping her students. Throughout her interview, she repeated one phrase— "student focused." She seemed more than happy to comply with new program requirements, but whether they involve technology or something else, she protects her priorities: "I will implement the changes, but in a way that doesn't upset the status quo, the students." Every change, whether large or small, has to, in Lauren's estimation, clearly benefit the students. She has to understand exactly how it will benefit them or she will balk, not out of a lack of enthusiasm but from an ethical concern. Lauren displays enthusiasm for new teaching methods even when she is terrified of them. In her mind, opportunities to try new things, to learn new methods of teaching, or to redevelop her curriculum end the day class starts. At that moment, her students demand her full attention.

The reflections of Shirley, Vivian, and Lauren echo Henry's two pertinent observations about the fire hose effect and the u-curve. But when we synthesize the experiences of these three late adopters with the portraits of other instructors, we find that the u-curve tells only part of the story. All three wanted, at least later on in their graduate careers, to contribute actively to the program. Shirley and Lauren found a niche they could become actively involved in. Each of the three found the technology daunting but had different reactions to it. Shirley decided it simply wasn't for her; Vivian admitted frustration but held out hope that she—or the program's website—could "evolve"; and Lauren found solace in small but steady victories, including learning how to use Blackboard and how to teach with blogs. Moreover, many of the other instructors, such as Audrey, also could be defined as late adopters.

So these categories—innovator, early adopter, early majority, late majority, and laggard—don't tell the whole story. Teachers move in and out of each category depending on how and when we define their relationships with technology. Moreover, when we talk about "innovation" in our program, we are talking as much about curricular innovation as we are about technological adeptness. And that, perhaps, is the major problem. We have treated curricular innovation and technological adeptness as synonymous rather than overlapping. Fortunately, instructors in our program have been able to make the distinction. This explains how Shirley could feel excluded by technology and yet not worry that it will inhibit her success as a teacher. And it indicates that Henry's u-curve could better be described as an imbalanced ecology, with many healthy subecologies that do not yet intermingle in a healthy way.

## CONCLUSION

Building a datagogical network is like running a marketplace, but the marketplace has been revealed as much more complex than we first realized. The exchange of ideas we expected between instructors was unequally distributed, with some teachers contributing a large amount and others only a small amount or none at all. But with the exception of Shirley, everyone we interviewed recognized the system as a good way to create a shared pedagogy, and even Shirley acknowledged its efficacy for some instructors. When measured by the degree to which users contributed to the website, success was mixed, with many instructors adding material only when required to or when specifically asked. But when measured by the degree to which instructors used our collaborative site and appreciated the shared pedagogy, our efforts have been mostly successful. We have learned that there is no single reason why people do not contribute, and that not every reason should be viewed as a negative. Certainly, the main website needs to be more intuitive for users like Vivian, whose hesitancy to contribute seems largely due to how intimidating she finds the technology. If given clearer instructions about how to share her material online—or clearly understanding that she can have someone else upload it—she would almost certainly participate more. However, for other users like Audrey, our website is simply a way to facilitate her teaching so that she can focus on being the best instructor and graduate student possible. Although she doesn't contribute regularly, she does take part in our shared curriculum. Her willingness to create a project, her attention to our shared project objectives when doing so, and her eagerness to share it with others demonstrate that we are effectively communicating the overriding vision of our program. That Audrey's project did not become fully implemented beyond her own classroom speaks to our need to simplify some of our collaboration processes but also to the dedication that some collaboration requires. And then there are instructors like Judy and Lauren, who are in some ways very similar. Judy is a beginning instructor with good technological skills, and Lauren is an experienced adjunct who is slowly learning PowerPoint. Both contribute in the ways they feel is best, with Judy loading only a few select favorite resources that she is confident won't "clutter up" the website and Lauren mentoring her peers on best teaching practices. Part of Judy's decision making is based on our software's weaknesses at organizing, but another part is based on where she is in her professional career and what she is comfortable doing.

This, then, is one way to understand all of these profiles: each instructor enters the program with his or her own level of both technological and professional experience, and this experience—as much as enthusiasm, interest, and a willingness to contribute—informs which percentage of the 80–20 dynamic they are in. What all of this suggests is that the success of a datagogical system can't be measured by the aggregate of what every instructor contributes to the site but rather by the individual talents and skills they bring to the program as a whole. A small group might upload the majority of the material, but each instructor plays an integral role in mentoring others, creating new projects, introducing new technologies, assisting others with technological problems, or simply uploading one or two great ideas. As Shirky writes, "You cannot understand Wikipedia (or indeed any large social system) by looking at any one user or even a small group and assuming they are representative of the whole" (127). What we have learned is that the degree to which a shared pedagogy is successful is only partially determined by who contributes what online. It's also about who shares that material offline, who mentors whom, and all of the countless conversations that would not have occurred without our online datagogy. In that sense, our website creates an atmosphere, one in which both online and face-to-face collaboration are much more possible than they otherwise would be.

**NOTE**

1. The *fire hose effect* is a generally used term, but it aptly describes what many of our interviewees describe indirectly.

## 5

## Agency in the Mentoring Program

*How does the mentoring program influence instructors' willingness to collaborate on our shared pedagogy? Why does the mentoring program's structure appeal to some instructors and push others away? What spaces can the mentoring program, with its scripted roles for instructors, offer for instructor creativity?*

BILLIE KEPT SHIFTING IN HER SEAT. She was working in a corner of the mentoring office while FYC staff members met to clarify the outcomes for a new writing project called "Agency and New Media," for ENC 1101. Even though Billie's back was to the meeting, her nervous energy was apparent as she shifted already organized papers into piles.

"What's up, Billie?" someone asked. "You don't like the new project?"

Billie sheepishly turned in her seat. She paused, took a breath, and said, "No, it's not the project really. It's the word *agency*, I guess. Or the idea behind the word." She looked around at the group. "I mean, you can't *give* someone agency. It doesn't work like that."

Billie was a respected graduate student instructor who had served as a mentor to incoming instructors for the past two years. Realizing that this was her opportunity to continue, Billie repeated, "It's just the word. And the way you seem to be throwing it around. You talk about giving people agency, when what you are talking about seems to have little to do with agency."

In many respects, Billie was right. The FYC staff had been using the word *agency* as an organizing principle for curriculum revisions. This new writing project was another example of our attempt to alert students to their shifting rhetorical powers when using various media for various audiences. Billie's comments reinforced John L. Schilb's 2009 MLA conference warnings about rhetoric and composition's "preoccupation" with agency (Jaschik). Our preoccupation finally forced Billie to speak up.

Billie continued, with quiet firmness. "Isn't agency always personal? It's the ability to act according to one's willingness to act. And I can't give that willingness to anyone, and neither can new media." Smiling, Billie swung back to her monitor.

Billie's desk was only a few feet away from the conference table in the mentoring office, where the FYC staff sometimes meets. Nine instructors, all mentors or facilitators in the FYC program, share the large office space. Each has carved out a niche in the office. Billie's space is sparse, save for a desktop file folder and a dangling corkboard. Pinned to the upper left corner of the corkboard is the 1968 image of two African American Olympians silently protesting their medal ceremony with clenched fists. Buttons declaring "Woman on the Loose," "End Occupation Now," and "Bail Out Main Street Not Wall Street" suspend exemplary student essays over her desk. On the bottom of her corkboard, a comic strip shows a character cutting down a beanstalk that takes him to big-box stores. Above the cartoon is a 2009 Provost's Teaching Award program: a single reminder of Billie's multiple teaching awards.

Billie's social concerns often creep into conversations regarding the FYC program, but she supports her arguments with philosophical or theoretical evidence. In later conversations, Billie integrated Louis Althusser's theories on structure, agency, and interpolation into her argument. She agreed that composition programs and new media tools *can* make spaces to encourage agency. "However," she added, "that is an ideal to be worked toward. And no matter what, the act, the agent's action, is always confined to the conditions in which the action is allowed." Institutional agency restricts actions because, according to Billie, "to suggest that an institution gives agency is to deny, or reduce, the individual's ability to act as her own agent. It also suggests that agency must be granted. It's not enough for me to be the one who can act. I must be given the ability to act, which ultimately denies my agency."

Billie's concerns resonated with us as we researched agency in the age of peer production. Through our research process, we had already started to question how to provide opportunities for our teachers to assume agency within a political institution like a state university. Billie's comments succinctly paraphrased our concerns. Heeding Schilb's warning about our preoccupation with agency, we wanted to tread wisely, not ignoring "state sovereignty in all its forms as somehow irrelevant" (Jaschik).

We raise Billie's story as an introduction to the complex forces at work surrounding the agency of any group or individual, whether student, instructor, or administrator. Agency is both allowed and reined in by institutional settings, and individuals both grasp agency on their own and are empowered by their membership in groups. It helps to imagine the interplay of these forces through the metaphor of a garden in a forest. In the untamed forest, individual plants could be described as having unprecedented "agency," with their ability to spread in any direction as far as their forms allow, but in a context of danger since at any moment that agency might be denied by the unprecedented growth of a neighboring plant. But imagine a clearing in that forest, with a number of garden beds constructed in it. Here, individual plants can flourish because the individual survival of each is attended to, yet they lack the ability to roam freely as they might in the forest. The clearing is both safer and less wild (less full of possibilities). If we see the university as a forest clearing, and individual garden beds as different departments and programs within the university, we can begin to picture the interplay of constraints and freedoms allowed by standardized systems. Billie was distressed that we would construct a bed for the students growing in it yet still rely on a discourse that pretends they have the freedom of the forest; she objected to language that ignores the borders constructing the garden bed and the ideologically driven clearing of the forest in the first place. And in another bed, our FYC mentoring program, individual teachers are encouraged to grow in reliance on one another's strengths, with one teacher's vine-like qualities wrapping around the corn-like qualities of another teacher, providing shade for the low-to-the-ground and wide-spreading qualities of another. To some degree, this collaborative growth occurs only because of the care given the plants within the structure of the garden bed—but it's true that many of these plants might do even better if allowed to spread wildly over the side of the bed and into the forest, without the hindrance of any institutional constraints.

Whereas the previous chapter looks at the exciting things that happen when vines creep outside of their prepared bed, this chapter looks at our mentoring program as an example of a structure built by the FYC program to foster growth. A garden bed both encourages and halts growth, structures and impedes it, reminding us of Stuart Blythe's assertion in "Agencies, Ecologies, and the Mundane Artifacts in Our Midst" that agency can be found within systems that both "constrain and enable" (173). We try to constantly shift our gaze between the two extremes, valuing the creative growth our teachers show that stems from our construction of the mentoring program even as we question the unavoidable ideological shaping that occurs when a garden is built and a forest is cleared. Billie's critique of our attitude toward student agency applies to our attempts to give teachers opportunities to assume agency: unable to simply *give* agency to teachers, as if we could stretch a vine to make it longer, we find ourselves *encouraging* them to feel empowered to share pedagogies, affect how composition is taught at RU, and speak actively on behalf of themselves, their fellow teachers, and their students. To do so, we have followed Peg Boyle and Bob Boice's model of "systematic mentoring," which begins with institutional rather than spontaneous mentoring; our program "systematically immersed newcomers in a structured support program and provided them with a sense of connectiveness" (173).

This chapter explores how our mentoring program, our face-to-face community, seeks to empower teachers both as individuals and as members of a larger pedagogical community in an age of peer production, when so many technological tools seem to offer the possibility of building relationships solely through computer interfaces. Though we discuss our own program, we suspect similar issues are at play in a variety of other "forest clearings," where institutional needs butt heads with individual and collective power. Our research examines the contradictions inherent in the mentoring program's ability to offer instructors the chance to assume agency within the confines of a top-down organization. Because support for the mentoring program comes from RU's General Education Council, we often feel that the program needs to satisfy measurable outcomes if we want funding to continue. And yet we also believe in the composition theorists' value of diversity of opinion; we often try to embrace conflict by making changes based on our instructors' concerns. In that sense, we make mentoring program changes not only by pushing but also through a mix of pushing and pulling. To illustrate how the program functions, and to investigate why the mentoring program, a series of primarily face-to-face initiatives, has effectively offered a space for instructors to exercise agency, we present ten perspectives of those who have participated directly or indirectly in our mentoring program. Our investigation discusses the kind of community the mentoring program has established, reactions to that community, the effects of agency on those who direct that community, and the range of contributions the mentoring program encourages instructors to make to the larger FYC community. Of course, as reporters on a program that evolved over three years, much about how we mentor instructors is still in flux as we adapt each year (and sometimes each month) to new instructors and new situations. We proceed, then, with a focus on the centripetal forces that impel instructors to our "gift culture" and how those forces, set by WPAs and the larger institution, can encourage or squelch agency.

## HOW IMPORTANT IS SOCIALIZING?

After two weeks of eight-hour days during our fall 2009 FYC orientation, it wasn't surprising to see a row of furrowed brows in the long coffee shop line. Too many workshops and training sessions can suck the life out of even the most dedicated teachers. But Shelly, a new instructor starting her master's program in British literature, was smiling. Reflecting on the orientation weeks, she mentioned that "everyone was so willing. To help me stop floundering about, you know. Someone was always there to answer my questions. And I guess I had a lot of questions. So it was nice that that someone was passionate." She described the FYC staff as "infectious." And like the caffeine in her nonfat sugar-free iced lattes that week, the orientation staff—primarily FYC mentors and facilitators—energized her, giving her a "desire to do well and to communicate and work with others." Shelly's response made us feel as though we had succeeded, tremendously.

The mentoring program has three goals: to improve student writing, enhance teaching strategies, and develop a cohesive, collaborative community. We succeeded marvelously on the last goal, as was evident by Shelly's enthusiasm and the attendance at the mentoring program's social gatherings. To help everyone relax after long orientation days, Eliza, the mentoring program director and second-year MFA student, would remind everyone to attend the evening's social event—pizza and beer, a movie screening, or dinner at a nearby restaurant. Even including bowling night, attendance at these social gatherings was surprisingly high: fifteen of the twenty-four new FYC instructors attended, on average, and eleven of the fifty-four returning instructors dined or bowled with us during the two weeks. But success on the other two goals is harder to gauge. Does getting instructors to hang out together create a cohesive and *collaborative* community? Does happy hour, softball, or kayaking inspire instructors to contribute to our shared pedagogy and to share their work with one another? Would drinking a beer or sweating through a home run help them recognize that our program relies on their contributions?

At the end of the coffee break during the last day of orientation, we all headed back to the final workshop, which began with an ice-breaker involving a ball of yarn, tosses across the room, and lots of knots. With this game, we hoped that Shelly and all the others could visualize how individual sharing was necessary for our community's success. But as the ball of yarn completed its crisscrossing through the room and we pulled tight on the strings, we weren't sure that everyone felt the tug. We weren't even sure whether Shelly, who admitted to feeling the tug, would continue to support our community throughout the semester and the upcoming year. Would instructors, whether through individual ambition or collective action, step up to effect change? Would they flourish in the garden that we had built for them, or would they creep over the edge and toward the freedom of the forest, to either flourish or die alone?

### ECOLOGIES OR GANGS?

The most obvious way that our mentoring program builds a garden bed is by constructing communities. By selecting six new mentors each spring, who in turn select at least three new instructors to mentor, we essentially frame incoming instructors' earliest professional relationships instead of allowing those with complementary interests and needs to naturally come together, as if we trained their vines up a frame instead of letting them explore. Or, to return to the metaphor of centrifugal and centripetal forces, our program asserts a centripetal force that draws attention to the centralized needs of the program whenever we hire new mentors. We try to ensure that mentors represent a variety of pedagogical styles, each with a special skill set. Over the past three years, we have moved from administratively assigning mentees to allowing mentors the chance to select their own mentees. We have also encouraged the mentoring director to select that year's mentors. This seems to have encouraged more lasting connections, but centrifugal forces are also always at work whenever we structure human relations—in other words, people naturally group themselves into communities of their choosing, whether through conscious choice or simple drifting. To some extent, we always grow into our own ecologies, shaping and being shaped by our connections in the network. No matter how satisfying new instructors find their relationships with mentors and co-mentees, they never grow perfectly into the shape their mentor has in mind—nor should we want them to.

The communities our instructors participate in range from face-to-face communities, such as shared office space or the required first-semester teaching practicum, to the online communities of the listserv and our program's websites. FYC is "like a neighborhood, of sorts," suggests Lisa, a second-year mentor. For her, the mentoring program is just one community within the larger FYC community. Amy, an RU adjunct and mentor, seems to agree; she says, "our writing program is like this campus: you can get lost, you can't just walk from one end to the other, you will never learn everyone's name, and there is always so much going on." She's right. We are a very large program. The sheer number of communities constituting RU's writing program can potentially feel alienating or decentralized. And yet Amy feels confident that her "mentees won't get lost, tangled, or drop the string," because they know she is their "first point of contact." Amy's vision of instructors "getting lost" has been known to happen. It's one reason why WPAs initiated the mentoring program: in the past, it was simply impossible for Joe to track more than eighty program instructors from semester to semester or year to year. Yet when some instructors start to flounder as the stress of the semester heightens, or fail to provide feedback on drafts before midterms, undergraduates bear the brunt of the consequences. Creating the mentoring program was one way to take the pulse of the whole program through structured communication—from mentees to mentors to the mentoring coordinator to the director of composition. But instead of individuals ferrying information to the top, relationships are formed throughout the program; Amy suggests that the mentoring program "puts a face to our massive FYC program."

But as we mentioned earlier using our garden metaphor, the "neighborhoods" often interact in ways other than how we structure them. Lisa's insights about our community being more like a neighborhood suggest that our multiple communities are led by gangs with allegiances to street corners, not to the neighborhood. Lisa's own allegiances are not clear. Often a critic of the overall curriculum, she deplores our reliance on technology. Her dislike for SharePoint extends to its use in the classroom; she argues that students, particularly disenfranchised ones, need to learn the fundamentals of composition before relying on technology. Lisa is a rhetoric and composition doctoral student in her third year at RU. Preparing to take her comprehensive exams, she is a thirty-year-old woman involved with graduate and Black Life organizations.

In many ways, Lisa gladly accepts opportunities presented through the FYC program, such as the opportunity to give her "tough love" presentation during orientation and editing ENC 1102's first textbook. But Lisa often pushes back and even refuses to comment when asked, "Does having a mentoring program make it easier for you to contribute? Encourage you in any way?" Obviously, Lisa contributes, but for what reasons? Her comments about our disconnected neighborhood hint at a buried hostility: "A fluid community could exist, but it is so divided." She goes on to state that many people, depending on their role in the program "can't come into certain parts of the neighborhood." She begins to divide people into "us" and "them" categories, waving her hand behind her, panning the mentors' shared office space. She claims in a murmur that "they see us as different. We are supposed to have the answers." When pressed, she labels "they" as everyone else: the mentees, the students in the practicum, the adjuncts, the visiting instructors, the returning instructors. "In our neighborhood, people have their role" and that, according to Lisa, influences levels of contribution. For the "adjuncts, this is their main source of income so they do what they have to," but the "graduate students contribute because it's part of their grade." Lisa concludes with the hope that there is a noticeable movement, "an effort," to reorganize the community so that people feel welcome coming into all areas of the neighborhood, and the mentoring program "could head that effort."

The message for WPAs is clear: structuring interactions between instructors through mentoring relationships—in large office spaces, in scheduled one-on-one and small-group mentoring—can have the effect of either bringing people into a shared commitment to the neighborhood at large or of pushing them aside into their individual street corners. Or, put another way, some plants grow into the structures we build for them while others reach out. And although our research helps us hear individual stories, attuning ourselves to their frustrations and praises, we can pull together no ultimate theory of structuring mentoring programs that accounts for the contradictory descriptions and advice. These contradictions were clearest in our conversations with Carol, a second-year PhD student in rhetoric and composition, and Brice, a first-year MA student in literature.

Carol's narrative, a typed response, reflects her positive reaction to the mentoring program:

> The mentoring program is indispensible because it helps new teachers get acclimated with the curriculum and the school itself. Eliza [the mentoring director] and the other mentors always seemed eager to help (and I probably should have taken advantage of their help more often). The apparent lack of pretense and elitism in the program is refreshing, from professors, staff and students. (I was afraid everyone would be wearing tweed jackets spouting obscure literary references, but everyone was so down to earth.) It seems like some members really put forth an effort to create the sense of community (the Thursday nights, which I can never go to because I always have class but wish I could), and perhaps some more opportunities for this would strengthen it further (I realize I can and should help with this instead of just being passive about it). I hope to become more of a member of this community as I continue through the program.

Carol's observations illustrate the complexities of her own comfort level, but always from a position of praise for the teaching community created through the mentoring program. In her reflection, she points to the "refreshing" aspect that encourages and respects new ideas. She seems to suggest that the mentoring program's structure allows new instructors to ease into the new curriculum. In her parenthetical statements, arguably the most telling in the response, Carol compares her own standing in the program to the community at large. Wanting to participate in communal events such as Sabbatical Thursdays, Carol champions more face-to-face communities. She also seems to realize her passive behavior about working to strengthen the community and concludes her response with a hope that she "becomes more of a member." Of course, a lot of instructors talk about wanting to be involved but then fail to lead or attend events once the semester gets going—but the general tone of respect for the mentoring program as a whole remains clear in this response.

Carol's recent "graduation" from the mentoring program could be a reason for her praise, because other instructors are not so positive about the program. For instance, Brice, a 2008 mentee, suggests that rather than being "indispensible," the mentoring program had no real influence on his program participation. Brice claims that the mentoring program was unsuccessful in fostering a sense of community because his group of fellow mentees was "too small." (Most mentoring groups consist of a mentor plus three mentees; Brice's had five people: his mentor and four mentees.) He says, "Moxley's practicum class [which most mentees take together during their first semester teaching at RU] facilitated a sense of community more so than the mentoring program." The 2008 teaching practicum comprised six times the number of participants in a mentoring group of four people. And yet while answering the last open-ended interview question, "Any thoughts on how the FYC program could offer more agency to instructors?," Brice seems to contradict himself, suggesting, "Maybe people could have small, informal meetings regarding specific issues that instructors deal with (problem students, swine flu, ineffective assignments, difficulties teaching certain projects, etc.)." Apparently, Brice didn't find in the mentoring program's structure of small, informal groups the same opportunities for agency that Carol found. Brice doesn't see the mentoring program as working toward developing community, but he does say that small face-to-face groups are one way to offer more opportunities to assume agency within our large program. Why would Brice claim that the mentoring program didn't provide him with access to agency when elsewhere he states that small groups might afford him this access? What causes the dissonance between Carol's and Brice's reactions to the same program?

The answer to these questions could ultimately be the differences in personality. Brice claims he would have assumed more agency, contributed more, if only his mentoring group had been more informal and dealt with timely pedagogical issues. Carol claims that the structure of the mentoring program and its emphasis on community make it invaluable for new instructors. And Amy confidently declares the mentoring program a beacon in the big city, one that keeps others from getting lost. These instructors have vastly different personalities: Brice is relaxed unless facing a poetry deadline; Carol is shy but grounded; Amy is confident concerning her developing teaching practices. But as FYC staff, we can't populate the mentoring program with Amy clones; the program has to run on more than personality. If we apply Lisa's reflections on why people contribute, it becomes clear that Brice felt he could best assume agency while participating in the practicum run by Moxley. He may have felt that these weekly meetings with the director of composition encouraged him the most to contribute—he could get instant feedback on his contributions and receive a grade for his work. The contributions he made outside the practicum "went unnoticed" and "often got buried on the website," so he "stopped bothering." Brice's need for Moxley's immediate feedback suggests that he never really subscribed to the program's philosophy, whereas Amy and Carol continue to contribute because they understand our program is larger than Moxley's personal philosophy. Instructors are integral to our program; their contributions often steer our evolving program. Ultimately, we needed Lisa's reflections to reach this conclusion. As the most outspoken instructor regarding our reliance on peer-production tools, Lisa proved that we need instructors and mentors who buy in to our gift culture, not just people with a certain personality type.

## MENTORING SPACES: OFFICES, HALLWAYS, AND ONLINE

Continuing the exploration of where mentoring programs exert centripetal force and where individuals shoot away from the center through their own centrifugal force, we discuss the spaces where mentoring happens. These spaces are sometimes constructed (a large, purposefully stocked office for mentors; online collaborative spaces) and sometimes random (conversations in hallways; other kinds of online collaborative spaces).

Five months after orientation, we asked Shelly, the enthusiastic coffee drinker, about the mentoring program and her contributions to the FYC program. She seemed caught off guard and a little guilty as she told us that she doesn't contribute to FYC's curriculum. When pressed, she fleshed out her answer: "I don't contribute to FYC because the primary way to do that is through the website, and I would rather have my teeth pulled than have to use that website. I don't think this is an issue of training—goodness knows we've had lots and lots and lots of training. I think the website is just fundamentally not user-friendly." As a new master's student in rhetoric and composition, Shelly brings lots of energy and new ideas to the program. At twenty-nine, she is a bit older than the other new MAs. When pressed for ways others could contribute that don't involve a degree in dentistry, Shelly reverted to discussing ways she *does* contribute: "I guess the only way I contribute to FYC is through the mentors then. They are, almost all, approachable, interested in making the program stronger, and perhaps most importantly, human beings instead of websites." Shelly explained her past semester's interactions:

> When the password for the quizzes was somehow changed, I went right to Eliza and she got Quentin to fix it. And then when the reader did not have any good readings for my project two option, I told my mentor and she put some on the website for me and everyone else. And when I didn't understand the historiography project, I went into the mentoring office almost daily to complain. Together we came up with lesson plans and they broke it down for me. I then went back to my office mates and shared with them.

Shelly's comments reveal much about the underlife in our program. As discussed in Chapter 4, *underlife*, Robert Brooke's term borrowed from sociology, refers to the ways in which individuals resist the identities prescribed to them by institutions or a program like ours, instead finding constructive ways to add to them. We get a sense through Shelly's comments of how underlife occurs in our program: after sharing her concerns with others in the mentoring office, she returns to her office mates with solutions. As instructors quip about technological issues in their shared office space or at social gatherings, they often manage to convert seemingly difficult problems into opportunities for conversation. Shelly admits that "complaining" often got her answers to problems other instructors would just ignore. Unintended relationships develop out of the mentoring program and the shared office spaces. Perhaps because Shelly is a bit older and a bit more outspoken, she asks questions others are afraid to ask. Her life as a mentee, then—the times when she is most actively being mentored in how to participate in our teaching community as well as when she's unofficially mentoring others—is defined by her relationship with two places: the large mentoring office, where she comes in search of human connections, and in her own office, where she shares her newfound knowledge. But the key to her role is that she clicks back to her office, briefcase in tow, to share with her less adventurous office mates. Shelly finds agency through interpersonal relationships and preplanned spaces, whether or not they have any connection to the age of peer production.

Shelly's craving for human connection and her perception that our websites are "fundamentally not user-friendly" contrast with Sam's experiences. Rather than through mentoring and being mentored in formally constructed office spaces, Sam's sense of agency comes from the enthusiasm for the program he found in his mentor, which transformed into an enthusiasm for sharing in online spaces—a very different model of teacher agency from that described by Shelly. Boasting about his contributions to the program, Sam rattles off the projects he's piloted and the lessons he's shared online: "I just can't help it. It's so easy. My students have to see the project and the lesson plan anyway, so I just upload it to CollegeWriting." Sam is a lanky, white twenty-three-year-old in his final year at RU, completing his master's thesis on contemporary American literature. Dressed in jeans and an open, long-sleeved flannel shirt covering a white Hanes T, Sam often gives off a relaxed vibe. When asked about the time it takes to make his curriculum contributions, Sam smiles and casually says that "Blackboard is the tool we should be complaining about. It's so closed compared to SharePoint and like twice the work." Sharing his daily lesson plans or even homework assignment reminders in Blackboard for both of his ENC sections means Sam would have to do it twice, once for each class. A course copy option is available in Blackboard, but he "would still have to click it and click what section and then what folder and then click okay." For Sam, "It's just not worth it." He contributes to the program because for him, using the FYC website saves him time: "I just send out one link, have to do it one time." But when discussing the mentoring program, Sam calls himself "an anomaly." He claims it was his mentor who "inspired" him to "want to give back because her energy for the program was infectious." She "really believed in this community, and then made me feel like a member of it. So she, then, couldn't help but believe in me. So I believe now and that's why I share." The formula seems simple enough.

Sam's enthusiasm for sharing online is rare. He reminds us that in some ways our FYC program's Web presence mirrors the mentoring program. Our initial interactive websites and the first year of the mentoring program were marked by an overly optimistic sense of "If we build it, they will come." We expected that giving instructors the technological tools to share lesson plans, write in collaborative wikis on topics of their choosing, and shape the curriculum online was enough to make them do so, much as we initially expected that simply assigning new instructors to mentors would automatically create relationships that would improve teaching abilities, trickling down to improvement in student writing. But in the 2008–09 school year, with eighty-three instructors, only seventeen instructors regularly logged in to the program's website. Six of those instructors are contributors to a majority of our writing projects, meaning they are already active contributors or have been on staff. While twenty-seven instructors applied to participate in the mentoring program over the past three years, fifteen of those were repeat applications—mentors reapplying for the same job. The two most recent mentoring directors were previously mentors. The five instructors who regularly attend the FYC staff meetings are the same instructors who edited our first student textbooks and wrote our two instructor manuals. Of the seven 2009 mentors, six have authored new projects, three have edited textbooks, six have contributed articles to our textbooks, and all have led workshops. Of the twenty-two most recent mentees, only twelve have repeatedly introduced discussion threads on our FYC listserv. The other ten have not contributed at all. And other than the obvious reason of being too busy or uncomfortable with the technology, we don't know why they have not participated.

Our point is that to encourage more people to share regularly, to encourage more participation in both Shelly's and Sam's styles, we have found it necessary to introduce increasing amounts of structure into the program. Online, this means giving various wiki spaces clear rhetorical purposes (such as our wiki glossary and collaborative rubric manual) and building the same kinds of document dropboxes and links lists on each major writing project's page, in the same places. In person, this means encouraging more people to meet up in collaborative physical spaces such as our mentoring office and more specifically defining the roles that mentors and the mentoring director are expected to fulfill each year—which we discuss in the next section.

### HAVING THE POWER: SELECTING MENTORS AND COORDINATORS

An enduring question for our program is how to select those chosen to be mentors, and once chosen, how to define their job. We see this as part of our overarching investigation into the centrifugal and centripetal forces of the mentoring program. Is it best to pick mentors who seem to be "inwardly focused," believing in the central goals and values of our peer-production model of a writing program? Or is it worthwhile at times to choose mentors who are centrifugally looking outward or even those hostile to our shared pedagogy? Could these outward-facing mentors help develop a healthy underlife? And when discussing the mentor job description, should the job exert a strong centralizing force so that all mentors are doing more or less the same kinds of activities and support, or should mentors be encouraged to cut loose and play by ear when encouraging and training their mentees?

Earlier, we described how Sam called himself an "anomaly" because his mentor's enthusiasm inspired him to want to share likewise. This label makes us wonder if our selection of mentors should be restructured. We initially selected mentors based not on their contributions to the program or their dedication to our values but on their willingness to be of service and their ability to work with others. Sam described how his mentor cared passionately about sharing pedagogical materials online, and that mentor's infectiousness has made the program better—not just because of her leadership as a mentor and her contributions to the program, but also through Sam's contributions and those of the people he went on to inspire. Yet "speaking purely anecdotally," Sam claims his "success with and enjoyment of the mentoring program seems to have been more the exception than the rule." He sees his mentor-inspired, peer-production-enabled agency as unusual, perhaps even not replicable. Moving from his story to the story of Eliza, our third mentoring director, complicates further the question of how individuals become inspired to contribute, and if they are more effective when inward facing or outward facing—if individuals can be labeled so simply at all.

"I am just making the decisions from now on," Eliza states with what appears to be a new-found confidence. She seems to hold her head a little higher, even if she does stumble over her next statement: "Well, I am making the final call on at least the small ones. The ones we have already decided on. Or, the ones that need to be decided right now, without our usual hourlong chat." As mentoring director, Eliza occupies a position that some instructors would never apply for and others would be envious of. The director works very closely with Joe and needs to be organized enough to keep up with him. The mentoring director also works as closely as possible with all of the instructors, whose desires often conflict. Therefore, Eliza needs to be able to convey programmatic changes to the masses as well as keep Joe informed about program underlife. Rather than act as a beat cop, Eliza is an intermediary between administration and instructors. The previous mentoring director often commented on how much more work she was able to complete once the mentoring program was initiated. The line of instructors outside her office door disappeared because instructors were able to take questions and comments to the mentors instead. Even though Joe's office door is open, many instructors, like Ashley, a new master's student in American literature, "do not want to bother him unless it's really important, like getting-fired important." Instructors feel more comfortable discussing issues with Eliza because she is viewed as a peer, and as mentoring director she can appropriately convey issues that need to be addressed by WPAs.

Our mentoring program does its best to resist a traditional top-down structure. Thanks to the program's open pedagogy philosophy and Joe's belief that those instructors "on the ground" should "call the war," the mentoring program is based on what Gail McGuire and Jo Reger have called "feminist co-mentoring" (54). In our program, instructors mentor instructors; after the first three years, we revised the program to consist of peer-to-peer relationships. Moving beyond reliance on rank or academic title, peers select mentors based on program contributions. This means that in our mentoring program it would not be unusual for MA students to mentor PhD candidates, adjuncts, or visiting lecturers. During the mentoring program's second year, our FYC staff realized that the mentoring director needed to participate in the selection of mentors. Having Joe relinquish that power associated with his position as writing program director allowed for a flood of changes, mainly stemming from the trust the staff shared. The second mentoring director, Taylor, was inspired by this power shift. She wanted to do the same by trusting her mentors to select the mentees they thought would best fit their mentoring community. Each incoming mentee was required to respond to a SharePoint survey consisting of questions pertaining to pedagogy, technology, and community. Mentors used those responses to select their mentees. Because of this gradual shift, both mentoring directors and mentors have been afforded an opportunity to assume agency.

When Eliza was selected to be the program's third mentoring director, the staff continued this practice of power sharing. Eliza has assumed agency by learning how to juggle administration goals with the wants of the instructors. Speaking of her growing collaboration skills, Eliza states:

> I just keep on working at everything, everyone, all at once. I have had to put my foot down with the mentors—some didn't want to meet every other week or do their scheduled presentations. The mentees seem to be so eager, to work and talk to me. Like how some come during my hours to get answers to a question? Sally just can't figure out the new project and I don't know what else to tell her. The other instructors have questions too. But they are comfortable enough to go on the listserv—like Don's response to project one. And then there's Moxley. I want to make sure I get all his stuff done, but that often changes. Right now, he assigned me the 1102 pedagogy book. That was something I definitely wasn't expecting to do.

Eliza's brief explication of her position might paint her as sullen, but as she rambles on about her dynamic director tasks, her sunny disposition doesn't fade. This statement, beyond masking how much Eliza enjoys her job, touches on the variety of tasks she must accomplish. A twenty-five-year-old student, Eliza always looks professional regardless of her duties for the day. She has almost completed her MFA fiction thesis and, after moving from FYC instructor to mentor, Eliza has transformed from a self-declared "terrified, inept instructor and community member" into "the boss." She "credits" the mentoring program with her new confidence: "I still don't really know why I initially applied [to be a mentor]. My first year was really, really hard. I didn't know how to be a teacher and a student at the same time. But then, after I applied and I got the job, I felt like I had something to offer. Like I could teach others to at least not be as afraid." Now in a position of power, Eliza can help to select the next mentoring director. But not all the mentors or even the previous mentoring director were aware of how their positions offered them agency or labeled them as "the boss."

Indeed, our mentoring directors have struggled with how best to use the power they have, which we see as disrupting a traditional hierarchy of mentoring (tenured faculty member to student). As the previous mentoring director, Taylor claims she was unaware of the power invoked by her position until she was barred from a graduate party. She was distraught that her position negatively influenced her reputation with incoming mentees; she had wanted the job as a way to connect with people, not be ostracized by them. When pressed for more information on her relationships with the mentees or the other instructors in the program, Taylor paused. It was obvious she was filing through memories of her past three years with the program: "I realized that because my name was on everything—emails, projects, 'homework,' assessment information—I couldn't be upset that they initially viewed me as someone with the power to fire them. That was the moment, I guess. The moment I realized that I actually had some power."

Recognizing her agency encouraged Taylor to continue working with the program: "No other program would allow us, as grad students, to get this close to the administrative level. We get to make textbooks, not just lesson plans." Offering new instructors the ability to get their hands dirty in administrative details such as writing technology fee proposals and revising assessment strategies seems to be the best way to offer spaces in which to assume agency. Eliza's speedy recovery from terrified teacher to the "boss" implies that properly designated roles for mentors and mentoring directors will push people toward engagement. So WPAs have redefined the once vague mentoring roles as specific, accomplishable tasks that entice more instructors to get involved. For instance, the initial mentoring job descriptions simply stated that mentors would meet with the mentoring director and their mentees biweekly. In addition to the basic confusion of whether *biweekly* meant meeting twice a week or every two weeks, mentors were unsure of agendas. The current job descriptions list general mentoring duties, such as "participating in Teaching Orientation, meeting regularly with mentees and the Mentoring Coordinator, observing mentee classrooms, participating in the FYC Practicum, creating assignments, assessments, and sharing information for the FYC program by adding projects, readings, and assignments to the [FYC] websites." The job descriptions also include a list of twelve very specific duties, such as

3. Meet at least once every two weeks, face-to-face, with mentees to
   - Discuss challenges they experience in their teaching
   - Review papers each has graded and/or revise lesson plans
   - Share weekly assignments
   - Complete Mentee Meeting Reports

WPAs are further experimenting with the new mentor roles by allowing mentors to select a program area for which they can develop resources. Mentors can choose to be responsible for ENC 1101 or 1102 resources and project pages, work as the practicum or assessment facilitator, become the library commons liaison, or even edit our monthly newsletter. Our success with more specific job descriptions allows WPAs to pinpoint programmatic areas in need of attention and then encourage mentors to take responsibility for those areas. Looking back to Shelly, who didn't even realize she was contributing to the program, we need to train mentoring directors and mentors to recognize and employ their agency within the program. When we become more specific about program goals, we can extend power to mentors by allowing them to select the contributions they want to be responsible for. As WPAs, we then need to hold instructors accountable for completing their selected program responsibilities.

## "EMBATTLED TENDENCIES":
### REQUIREMENTS AND PERCEPTIONS

Making sure that instructors are aware of their opportunities to assume agency has been a focus for the mentoring program. Yet, as soon as WPAs try to offer these opportunities within the confines of a structured mentoring program, contradictions arise. Any time we asked questions about how the mentoring program worked as a centripetal force, how it followed the pattern set up by the administration, we found evidence of ways in which the mentoring program was also boundary breaking, suggesting a centrifugal force. Bakhtin reminds us, "It is possible to give a concrete and detailed analysis of any utterance, once having exposed it as a contradiction-ridden, tension-filled unity of two embattled tendencies in the life of language" (272). Surely this description extends beyond the tendencies of individuals struggling to carve out individual agency in a context of administrative control. For example, Jacob, a visiting instructor, can often be found grading papers by a window in the corner of the new student center, which is brightly lit and a good fifteen-minute walk from Cooper Hall, where Jacob teaches. He doesn't have office mates to share with and thus best expresses how the mentoring program represents embattled tendencies. At age thirty-three, Jacob was hired last-minute as a visiting instructor to teach four sections of ENC 1102. He honestly admits that he doesn't contribute to the program in any way: "There are a number of reasons, but I think the most important is that I teach four classes, and I have little time to do anything not directly related to the day-to-day affairs of the courses that I teach." The busy factor affects the majority of our instructors. During orientation and throughout the practicum, graduate student instructors are repeatedly reminded by Joe and the graduate director to concentrate on their own studies, that teaching is just a ten-hour-a-week appointment and they should focus on the classes they are taking, prepare conference presentations, or flesh out their CVs with publications. Sometimes that reminder privileges personal success over FYC student success. And the ten-hour-a-week time restriction often conflicts with the reality of grading three drafts of three major writing projects. Adjuncts and visiting instructors like Jacob maintain busy schedules that might not include graduate homework or publications but do include teaching multiple sections for financial reasons. Yet Jacob also doesn't get involved with the mentoring program. When reviewing his interactions with the mentoring program, he declares that he "had few interactions" with his mentor, but the first one must have had the most impact because he discusses that one in depth, reporting, "The first time I ever met her, during one of the orientation sessions, she expressed her doubts about whether or not I was prepared to teach the classes I was assigned to teach. This was discouraging, and it made me feel like my contributions would not be welcome." Knowing there are at least three sides to every story, it is quite possible that Jacob's mentor simply wanted to stress the difficulties he would face as an adjunct, teaching four sections and arriving late for orientation. But regardless of his mentor's intention, Jacob purposely places himself in the 80 of the 80–20 rule: he does not contribute because he felt that what he had to offer was not welcome. After reviewing the archival data, we concluded that Jacob wasn't being flippant about his lack of contribution. Not once in his two years at RU has he submitted anything to the listserv. He attended one Policy Committee meeting but has never submitted lesson plans, contributed to instructor-edited textbooks, offered revisions to projects, logged in to our teaching website, or applied for any new positions.

Lisa, who earlier discussed the mentoring program's neighborhood allegiances, seems to feel similarly about the mentoring program. Lisa also spends her time as far from Cooper Hall as possible. She discusses how our program's reliance on technology alienates instructors who are not technologically advanced enough to know how to upload files or those who forget log-in information and can't respond to program surveys. Her reaction to technology is one reason the mentoring director selected her for a mentoring position. At the time, it seemed reasonable that at least some incoming instructors would feel an aversion to technology, and Taylor wanted to make sure those instructors could find an allegiance within the mentoring program. Because of the focus on technology, Lisa claims, neither the FYC program nor the mentoring program "treats instructors as professionals," and according to her, "in order to act professionally, we must be treated so. In order to contribute to the profession, teach us as such. Make us come to regularly scheduled faculty meetings." From this statement, it's obvious that Lisa, like Carol, desires more face-to-face communities. From her point of view, Lisa isn't treated professionally when the FYC staff makes curriculum decisions without instructor advice. She also thinks that "when [instructors] are given the opportunity to make decisions or contribute, those opportunities often get undermined because of miscommunication. Project proposals won't be accepted; textbook table of contents change at the last minute or new lesson plans are not needed because WPAs changed projects without telling anyone. That is what makes me not feel like a professional, like a respected teacher in academia." For instructors to feel agency within the age of peer production, Lisa needs WPAs to set clear limits: "You can only be empowered when you know your limits." Lisa wants to teach instructors to be empowered within the limits of the hierarchical university institution. A monthly faculty meeting would be a "quick fix." At the meeting, "everyone would be told what's going on; they could have a voice" and offer opinions on how various committees move forward with new projects, book adoptions, or technology. For Lisa, our open-door FYC Policy Committee meetings do not encourage contribution, because they "feel closed-door." Chuckling, Lisa claims that even though she is on the committee, she doesn't go: "So why would those not on the committee go?" "At those meetings," she says, "people just report what decisions have already been made. There is no dialogue, so why should I contribute? What can I add?"

The striking similarities between Lisa's and Jacob's tones are nothing compared to the stark contrast between their contributing practices. Whereas Jacob happily isolates himself, Lisa has taken advantage of every opportunity the mentoring program has afforded her. To date, she has mentored for two years, authored three new projects, revised two old projects, submitted lessons to pedagogy handbooks, added links to the project pages, participated in listserv conversations, and edited the ENC 1102 textbook. Lisa's criticism of the mentoring program and the larger FYC program has only pushed WPAs to work harder to revise our program.

## CONCLUSION

The results of our research seem to suggest that Billie's initial reservations about agency were correct: as WPAs, we can set up a structured garden bed with only the hope that we will create spaces in which instructors can assume agency. For interpersonal reasons, some people may reject our invitations to assume agency. And for some, the refusal to contribute can simply be about personality, regardless of interpersonal relationships. The mentoring program, according to Amy and Eliza, does create spaces for agency. And from what we have learned through Shelly's and others' comments regarding our peer-production tools, the mentoring program is necessary—without the face-to-face community, our program would reflect only those voices, like Sam's, who are comfortable with peer-production software. Our mentoring program enables those not technologically advanced the same opportunity to contribute to the program.

Each year the mentoring program evolves in ways that reflect the findings of our larger study: the more democratic the mentoring program becomes, the more defined the mentor role becomes. We have learned that, as with the larger program, we cannot just give people a space or log-on information and hope they contribute. Instead, we need to give people the chance to feel empowered by offering them specific and defined tasks to accomplish. When we began the mentoring program, this seemed like a contradiction of sorts, but now we realize that each person involved needs guidelines. Joe no longer selects the mentoring director or assigns mentees to mentors; now, each member selects appropriate colleagues and job roles. The mentoring program was instituted in 2007 so that qualified, willing instructors could focus on creating a reasonable curriculum. Before the General Education Council accepted our proposal, our larger program had no funds to focus on curriculum, no resources to develop curriculum, and no time to explore assessment strategies. Thanks to the mentoring program's success, we have a continuous source of funding to focus on curriculum and assessment revisions. The mentoring program has also been an incredible crowdsourcing outlet—those instructors who subscribe to our program philosophy and those who do not equally provide suggestions for improvement.

# 6

## Agency, Peer Production, and University Composition Programs

*What have we learned? What can other writing programs learn from our messy attempts to use social media to peer-produce a standardized curriculum? Have we identified instances of emergent intelligence? What does our story suggest about the changing face of agency, control, and collaboration in the twenty-first century—not just for WPAs, but for the members of any complex, networked group?*

INSPIRED BY ARGUMENTS THAT peer-production technologies facilitate an emergent intelligence and democratize the construction of knowledge (Benkler; Surowiecki), and that crowds of teachers can be smarter than any single teacher (Moxley, "Datagogies"), we began "crowdsourcing" the development of our curriculum in 2004. Over the next five years, we found that a small number of our teachers played a disproportionately large role in developing our curriculum and program policies. We checked our experience against the experiences of other online communities and found that our experiences weren't unusual: a small group of people commonly do the lion's share of the work. Peer-production sites are guided not so much by the wisdom of the crowds as by the "wisdom of the chaperones" (Wilson). The gulf between our desire to engage as many composition instructors as possible in our collaborative effort and our actual experiences inspired us to conduct a yearlong qualitative study of our own writing program, interviewing teachers, reviewing correspondence such as listserv emails and newsletters, and analyzing use of our numerous websites. Our goal was to understand how peer production influences the agency of teachers and writing programs, and to perhaps provide a road map for other university writing programs to follow as they begin experimenting with social media and peer-producing shared pedagogies.

Following our research, we have come to a more nuanced understanding of agency and of how to facilitate a gift culture. This means, in part, that we have rejected more universal claims that peer production invariably disrupts traditional power hierarchies and democratizes the construction of knowledge. As demonstrated by our research, for example, some instructors will reject any use of peer-production tools, preferring instead to do the minimum necessary with technology. To some graduate students and adjuncts, any forced interaction online can feel stifling and disempowering. For others, lack of participation is tied to other commitments: some of our graduate students may be taking three courses, teaching two for RU, and perhaps teaching two, or even three or four, additional courses for a local college or global online university. Even those who aren't resistant to new technologies may reject involvement with these tools for any number of reasons: because the university reward system praises individual scholarship rather than the development of a university's writing program (Boyer; Winston), because of time constraints, because a particular use of a technology advances the agency of writing program administrators over the agency of an instructor—the list goes on. That said, many of our instructors do find agency and voice by using peer-production tools or by working with friends or WPAs to upload content and edit existing content and policies. In our community, we see growing evidence of a thriving environment of networked, peer-produced knowledge. While our experiments with social media as a way to develop a shared curriculum might not capture the imagination of all faculty, some of our efforts have been transformative and empowering.

How, then, should we view agency when some individuals feel empowered and others feel silenced by the same actions? We view agency as neither platonic nor ubiquitous; instead, we believe the ability to effect change within an institutional educational context in the twenty-first century depends largely on an understanding of how individuals interact with one another (both in face-to-face and online contexts) and define themselves and their community. Somewhat surprisingly, we have found that agency is not necessarily bounded exclusively by one's ability to use technologies, but by one's network of online and face-to-face relationships. Hence, rather than looking at agency in a monolithic way, as something one either has or doesn't have, or as intimately tied to technology adoption, we view agency as contingent, context specific, and process driven. Perhaps not surprisingly, given our perspective as technorhetoricians, we view agency as a rhetorical construct that occurs among people in a networked community—an ecology—as they engage in various activities. Note, for example, that from a bird's eye perspective our writing program's use of the rubric tool advanced the agency of WPAs at the expense of the teachers, while our peer-production site undermined the authority of WPAs, providing teachers with a public forum to debate the logic and efficacy of proposed program changes. We have also come to see how our mentoring program, websites, and online rubric each form competing but also complementary subcommunities. The mentoring program acts as both an escape hatch for those who don't buy into our peer-production model and a periscope for those who want to participate online but need guidance. The online and offline communities described in Chapter 4 illustrate how instructors with widely different technological predilections can find their way to our websites through many different paths, and can find their way into a collaborative group even without those sites. It's the interplay of all these factors that foreground the varied possibilities of agency that can exist within a community.

In the twenty-first century, then, agency depends largely on an understanding of how individuals interact with each other and define themselves and their community. Though chaotic, these individuals and communities find ways to interact with each other, moving like vines into and out of each other's spaces, messily engaging with each other, but always growing, winding towards or away from different technologies or institutional constraints, bunching into the spaces created for them or breaking barriers—an emerging, organic, growing ecology of networks, friendships, and hubs for innovation, reflection, and critique. The agency of a complex group using peer-production tools is ecological in nature: organized, yet chaotic; individualized, yet harmonized.

### AGENCY FROM AN ECOLOGICAL PERSPECTIVE

Our concept of agency has come to mirror Porter et al.'s model of institutional change, which associates change with the rhetoric employed by the people who constitute an institution. We are inspired by the idea that "[t]hough institutions are certainly powerful, they are not monoliths; they are rhetorically constructed human designs (whose power is reinforced by buildings, laws, traditions, and knowledge-making practices)" (611). More specifically, we suggest that agency emerges from the interplay of the following major dynamics:

1. the dual roles of individual and communal agency
2. the tensions between face-to-face and online communities
3. the tensions between a tool's ease of use ("the Facebook effect") and its complexity ("the fire hose effect")
4. the degree to which people are empowered or not empowered by their adoption or rejection of technologies
5. the tension between faculty members' need to develop a stable pedagogy versus the need to revise a curriculum or even develop an alternative curriculum in response to ongoing datagogical feedback
6. the tension between the marketplace of ideas and the need for administrative control

Note that these are *tensions* and *dynamics*, not *always-present truths*. As overlapping possibilities, these traits describe the trajectory we've observed in twenty-first-century communities, but we recognize that they may appear differently in other landscapes. They're also *ecological*, a metaphor we're attracted to for its complex relationships, wherein small changes can ultimately yield tremendous change. George Siemens describes ecologies in this way:

A hiker entering a new territory would think it foolish to settle on a simple, myopic, diluted definition of the ecology. Instead, the rich space is explored for plant and animal life, streams and lakes; sounds and smells. Any singular definition of the landscape would fail to define the whole. Each definition of the landscape becomes valuable when it abandons pretences of being the only one and acknowledges other perceptions. This does not embrace relativity. . . . It does, however, embrace diversity, acknowledging that many different views exist, and different ones will be more applicable in different situations (each context may better align with one particular view, eliminating the notion of equal validity of all views in a particular context). (13)

From Siemens's perspective, agency ecologically emphasizes the rich diversity of individuals making up a community, the many different actions that can lead to individual and communal agency, the value of considering power from a variety of perspectives, and even the existence of best answers to certain problems that threaten the livelihood of the whole.

A crucial aspect of this ecology is found in the experiments practiced by the people on the ground doing the work—in our case, FYC teachers. Some of the most interesting projects begin as individual experiments; some of the best advice about the online rubric began with Paulo's inspired insight, and the insights of a few key instructors have often informed our summer overhauls of the curriculum. But even though each of these instances demonstrates the spark that can arise from a single stone, without a stack of kindling, the flame dies. Paulo had a plan of action concerning the best way to develop My Reviewers, our online rubric tool, and Audrey proposed a provocative new composition assignment, but their ideas would have provided little programmatic warmth without an institutional network to nurture the flames. This is another way of saying that instructors as autonomous individuals have limited agency; it often doesn't extend beyond the classroom, and this freedom belies the many programmatic, department, school, and university requirements that limit teacher independence.

Without much dialogue between other teachers—that is, without discussions between teachers about the desired outcomes of particular classes, about ways to scaffold outcomes from class to class, and about larger, programmatic outcomes—teachers and students lack a coherent narrative, which as Gerald Graff has noted can result in educational malaise ("Why Assessment?"). Students move from class to class without making meaningful connections between these different subecologies, regarding education as a matter of regurgitating material that is quickly forgotten. The current reliance on courseocentrism results in a mere veneer of instructor autonomy—an autonomy that ultimately undermines our authority and the educational process. Think of a fist thrust through a bucket of water; the fist is impeded by nothing but makes no permanent impact. To make an impact, we need to come together.

So agency needs to be viewed more holistically, as an integration of the individual and the community, as something that occurs when people interact with one another around goals and activities, as in Siemens's "rich space" for exploration and action by many different agents. Whether in the realm of business, politics, law, or community activism, people effect change by becoming part of a community, organization, or institution. These larger communities have the potential to represent the voices of those who otherwise might not be heard, to provide a forum for people to share their opinions and to be informed and shaped by their members. This interplay between individual and communal agency works similarly in educational contexts. For instructors to effect change and influence their students, peers, and universities, they need to have both personal autonomy and communal identity. By finding a way to encourage both, writing programs can discover an attentive audience and possibilities for effecting real change through a larger community. While the idea of individual agency may seem at odds with collaboration, Blythe reminds us that individual agency can exist within the agency of a group: "Agency involves a 'lack of constraint,' by which people are free to make meaningful decisions and take personal action; simultaneously, it involves the ability to function 'as part of something larger'" (173). We're drawn to this vision of individual and communal agency overlapping in productive, empowering ways.

As we shift our view from the perspective of the individual factors making up our ecology to the wider picture of how they interact, we recognize another aspect of agency—a dialectical relationship between the individual and the program. From the individual's perspective, this relationship opens up a space for a "redress of grievances," to borrow a phrase from our Constitution's First Amendment. Discussion boards, wikis, open-door committee meetings, mentoring availability, options to revise or create assignments (for others to use), all create an atmosphere of accountability on the part of administration. We realize this might seem overly optimistic, and we don't mean to suggest a Rockwellian scene of democracy in its most perfect form. What we do mean to suggest is that we value programmatic accountability, and we have experienced the potential for peer-production technology to set a creative and positive tone. This wide-lens view of our ecology empowers administrative leadership to represent faculty, which can enhance the reputation of a program, provide additional funding, and help to define a program's goals or objectives to the larger department, college, or university. My Reviewers, and the rich assessment information it provides, has elevated the status of the writing program within our university and helped us receive grant money to obtain teaching resources (office computers, books, printers, a separate office suite for our administrators and mentors, etc.), invite guest speakers, and hire additional mentors or technology collaborators. Our mentoring program has opened up new lines of employment for graduate students, earned course reductions, and provided opportunities for professional development. These types of representation—what some might call "branding"—can give a community a sense of its own boundaries, its own belonging. One exemplar of this is Purdue University's Online Writing Lab, which has a well-earned national reputation for excellence. This type of reputation can only help to create a sense of communal identity. That's what we're working toward here at RU—a sense of community that inspires people to work together.

## HEURISTIC QUESTIONS OF AGENCY

Our model of agency calls for individuals to "kairotically" scope out when and how action should occur. With that in mind, our theory should be seen as an inquiry-driven heuristic rather than a philosophy carved in stone. Our heuristic especially applies to anyone who teaches in or administrates a large writing program with a diverse student body and a faculty that regularly rotates in and out of university programs (adjuncts, lecturers, and graduate students). Those individuals should consider the following nonexhaustive questions when deciding how to exercise agency, or when assessing the agency of teachers and administrators in an existing composition program:

- Are teachers informed about the institutional responsibilities of the writing program, especially in terms of assessment, service to other departments, or national reputation?
- What procedures or avenues are in place for teachers to communicate problems with administrators? How can peer-production technologies be used to create these avenues? How can face-to-face relationships be used to create them?
- In what ways has professional development been defined within the writing program among instructors? How do those definitions reinforce or undermine an understanding of individual and communal agency? How do those definitions encourage formal or informal mentoring, curriculum sharing, and grade norming?
- In what ways do teachers interact using technologies that are not institutionally supported (e.g., Facebook, instant messaging, text messaging)? What does this say about their values and about their practices? What does this say about their comfort with technology?
- What types of explicit or implicit messages are relayed about a program's definition of community to instructors, the university at large, and the professional community? Does the writing program provide awards for service, curriculum development, mentoring, and teaching?

• In what ways is a program responding to new technological opportunities? In what ways is it critical of new technologies? In what ways is it in process?

## IMPLICATIONS

The changing face of agency has wide-ranging implications for the day-to-day specifics of the life of a writing program using peer-production tools.

*1. Peer-Production Tools Enhance the Communal Agency of the Writing Program.*

Our research results demonstrate that university writing programs can benefit from having an interactive Web portal—a teaching/learning/writing space that allows users (teachers, administrators, and students) to author, edit, and discuss documents. Peer-production tools can provide the intellectual space needed to coordinate communal efforts to help programs create program goals, activities, and assessment measures, which for us has resulted in significant internal funding. As a result, we have been able to hire more teachers, ensure the supervision and mentoring of new teachers, and develop new assessment measures to better understand student progress in light of our course objectives. Additionally, with approximately 200 unique users each day exploring our website, we know our curriculum is transparent—that other professors in other disciplines can quickly find out what our outcomes are—which enhances our credibility campuswide.

*2. Peer-Production Tools Empower Teachers, but Teachers Need Guidance.*

From our study, we have learned that the route to teacher agency is often indirect, at times involving administrative actions that seem to undermine academic freedom. We believe that the advent of peer-production tools enables the creation of flexible intellectual spaces for WPAs and instructors to work together to empower teachers in the classroom and empower writing programs as they compete for grants and funding. Because these tools so easily enable teachers to share resources and collaborate on an outcomes-based curriculum, they can help convert "isolated, privatized classroom[s]" into "collective structures of discourse and representation" (Graff, "It's Time"). Though peer-production tools are not a panacea, we have found that they can further a WPA's goal to develop a standardized, shared pedagogy that is open to constant debate and revision—a datagogy. We've also found that administrators should explicitly communicate to graduate students the professional development opportunities connected with contributing to and sharing within the program: i.e., the opportunity for vita lines, especially in terms of assessment, curriculum development, and service.

Peer production and social media can tear down the walls that atomize each classroom and by doing so yield many beneficial effects of transparency. They enable the university community to better understand what happens in these courses, thereby increasing the likelihood of funding; they allow WPAs to better assess the writing program (since instructors are sharing assignments and resources) and therefore improve it based on information gathered; they open the classroom doors, enabling teachers and students across sections of the same course to share writing projects and resources. Rather than limiting academic freedom and authority, social media and peer production can provide agency for individual classroom instructors, allowing them to shape the direction of an entire writing program.

However, we have found that this vision is rarely seen the same way by all the parties involved. Our research shows a reluctance among our instructors to work together on collaboratively authored documents or to work together to produce revisions to official projects, a reluctance that extends even to those who are active uploaders of material to our websites. Judy, for example, is one of the "Young and the Restless" who dives into peer-production tools ahead of everyone else, yet she hesitates to share much of her work with anyone beyond her students, reporting that it's not good enough yet. Others are too busy to work together, or they simply don't see the benefit of working through the inevitable difficulties. (We admit that as researchers we occasionally struggled with day-to-day misunderstandings while collaboratively conducting this research study, even as dedicated as we are to the theory of collaborative knowledge generation.)

We suggest creating collaborative spaces with a clearly defined structure to coordinate contributions and direct people's individual talents. Develop small committees with focused tasks. Rather than worry about each teacher within the same group of "contributors," recognize the different skills and needs of each faculty stakeholder group. For instance, from this push to create constructive collaborative spaces, we have learned to offer beginning MA students the security needed to ease into a collaborative atmosphere and to give experienced adjuncts the chance to draw from their own lesson plans. We've also discovered the value in making curriculum collaboration an activity that takes place in face-to-face as well as online spaces, such as by convening a number of subcommittees with very specific tasks. This involves scaffolding collaboration by creating small teams with clearly defined goals. We also recommend that when creating a wiki for lesson plan collaboration, first populate the wiki with expectations and clearly marked spaces for anticipated conversations. This should ease worries about how and where to begin collaboration, especially for new instructors—which helps build the visible mainframe of composition pedagogies online, which in turn helps boost the program's reputation among the other departments at the university.

### 3. The 80–20 Rule Underrepresents Sharing and Collaboration.

Following our qualitative research, we have come to realize that our community is far richer and more dynamic than we originally believed. The 80–20 rule applies to our teachers' program contributions but insufficiently explains their layers of sharing. At first glance, only a small number of our faculty upload course materials to shared Web spaces, but as we look more closely at the daily activities of the supposedly inactive 80 percent, we see bustling movement, interaction, and sharing happening under the radar.

Even those who do not actively participate online share in the halls, through personal emails, and in their shared offices; they promote helpful materials that have been uploaded by someone else. Many other instructors who seem to be avoiding full engagement in the program are gaining professional experience by being attentive but not interactive users of our website. This is especially true for beginning MA students or adjuncts who are technological late adopters. For instance, Tony, Judy, Claudette, and Audrey each expressed the desire to share, collaborate, and form a subcommunity amongst themselves, and Tony and Judy both conveyed their eagerness to borrow from uploaded material but also an initial hesitation to upload because of their inexperience as teachers (see Chapter 4). Other, more experienced instructors such as Vivian and Shirley were intimidated by their technological inexperience, yet both reported that they slowly acclimated to the online community, navigating the site and downloading and uploading materials. And still others like Marlene fit an entirely different profile; she is a highly experienced adjunct who quickly adopted the datagogical model and identified herself as an early adopter/innovator, but she felt alienated from the face-to-face interactions many graduate students participated in. As an adjunct, she felt isolated from what she perceived to be a cliquish group of graduate students. What these profiles show us is that a culture of sharing is indeed alive, even if we don't always see evidence in the shared spaces online where we most expect and hope to see it. It also reinforces the reality that our faculty do not neatly divide between technophiles and technophobes, collaborators and individualists, or any other easy dichotomy. Instead, we have found that a successful datagogy forms as many connections between people and subcommunities as possible. These connections come through online interfaces but also through face-to-face interactions such as committees, mentoring programs, practicum classes, parties, colloquia, and even shared office space.

We have found that balancing face-to-face and online networks is essential for a datagogical community. As our interviews have reminded us, our teachers are diverse; they respond to different types of environments and range from innovators and early adopters of technology to late adopters and laggards. Thanks to our mentoring program, some of our laggards are our most influential creative contributors. As our research also indicates, some of our strongest mentors and some of our most involved instructors were late adopters who shared and collaborated offline. Moreover, some instructors would upload material to our website but then share that they had uploaded with friends via face-to-face networks rather than wait for others to find their new contributions. In terms of agency, this blend of environments empowers instructors who might otherwise feel unable to act. Not encouraging this mix might prevent instructors from sharing teaching resources and undermine the efforts toward shared pedagogy. We've come to deeply appreciate the many people who do contribute to our program, and we have become attentive to the more circuitous ways in which ideas bubble to the surface. This tells us that our gift culture is like an iceberg, with the majority of the giving happening beneath the surface. We have increasingly invested in the face-to-face side of our teaching community in a number of ways: a strong, mandatory two-week orientation each year that includes both training and community-building activities; a mentoring program that emphasizes small-group discussions throughout new TAs' first semester of teaching; and a peer-led mentoring program that helps to cut down on hierarchical shyness. Given the successes of this program, we are clearly in support of similar mentoring programs at other universities.

We cannot argue that it logically follows that other university writing programs should require frequent face-to-face meetings. Our experience, however, has been that some instructors have difficulties attending these meetings during the semester because they frequently teach at other community colleges and universities or have other responsibilities such as daytime jobs in local high schools. Hence, WPAs might require attendance at three out of five semester meetings to regularly discuss changes made to the curriculum or program technologies. Ideally, WPAs can find funding to compensate instructors for these meetings, which could also include mini-technology training sessions that address common user errors or software bugs. More likely, programs could use instructional technology such as podcasts, vodcasts, or screen videos to provide guidance to busy adjuncts and graduate students.

*4. Peer-Production Tools in a Workplace Setting Must Account for Motivations Different from Those on the Web.*

This study looked at the use of peer-production tools in a workplace context—the intellectual space of teachers in our writing program—as opposed to the nonhierarchical writing spaces that are open to everyone and geographically dispersed, such as Wikipedia or Newsvine or Writing Commons. Nonetheless, we found many of the same advantages of peer production that Web 2.0 theorists have celebrated, including greater agency for teachers, emergent intelligence, and the wisdom of crowds or the power of crowdsourcing—or, in our case, teachersourcing. But the motives that drive faculty to contribute are more varied and complex than exist in nonworkplace environments.

Just like contributors to peer-production sites such as Wikipedia, some of our teachers share for the reasons commonly cited in discussions of peer production, which "rang[e] from the pure pleasure of creation, to a particular sense of purpose, through to the companionship and social relations that grow around a common enterprise" (Benkler and Nissenbaum 403). Once empowered with the chance to change the curriculum, some instructors, like Shelly, felt the need to improve the website, share classroom activities, or clear up any confusing language on the project pages. And there are always those who continue to share out of goodwill (especially when the Web interface eases the process).

But teachers reported sharing the most during the graduate teaching practicum because it was required, because they were part of a structured environment in which sharing and uploading were discussed, and perhaps most important, because their contributions were quickly noticed. Many of our instructors reported that they were hesitant to share information, edit online material, upload lesson plans, or contribute to online discussions after the practicum. Many teachers reported a type of self-fulfilling prophecy of community apathy. Much like a bank run, where every depositor races to withdraw their savings when they hear of others doing the same, our graduate students would at times abandon our online resources after the practicum when they saw their peers doing the same. From their perspective, they needed a reasonable assurance that their work—both the lesson plan and the act of uploading—would be noticed by others. When they experienced feedback from peers or recognition from administrators, they reported contributing more both online and offline. Often this feedback came in the form of face-to-face meetings, and our site became just one of many avenues for sharing information, the others existing in the halls, offices, and classrooms underneath the radar of administrative notice.

We've found that any activity, interface, or subcommunity that recognizes contribution and ensures that sharing will be used in practical ways by others will increase the probability that faculty will share. This is another reason face-to-face events such as brown-bag lunches, colloquia, and orientations are so important. Splitting instructors into smaller grading groups or sharing groups may also increase a collaborative atmosphere by giving the members of a community faces and names they can relate to. Rather than uploading something for eighty instructors, uploading for four or five fellow mentees (see Chapter 5) or four or five fellow graduate students provides a real sense of recognition and reward, as well as the tangible knowledge of who the contributor helped. Small collaborative teams can therefore play a very helpful role.

### 5. Avoiding the "Black Box Fallacy": Face-to-Face Collaboration Works in Concert with Online Communication.

Through our research, we have learned that online communities do not foreshadow the elimination or even waning importance of face-to-face collaboration. As Shirley and Lisa suggest (see Chapter 4), face-to-face communication is still the exclusive type of interaction for many of our instructors, and it is undoubtedly privileged by all of our faculty, not to mention our administration. Instead of thinking about peer-production technologies as displacing more analog forms of professional interaction, it's better to think in terms of layering, one layer or media platform placed on top of another. Henry Jenkins refers to the false assumption that we are inevitably marching toward an all-purpose, ubiquitous piece of technology that can be used for everything as "the black box fallacy," explaining that "part of what makes the black box concept a fallacy is that it reduces media change to technological change and strips aside the cultural levels" that inform decisions made by communities and individuals (15). We need to think in terms of ecology, that "old media never die—and they don't even necessarily fade away" (13).

### 6. Simplicity, Not Content, Is King.

Learning how to avoid "the black box fallacy" reminded us that simplicity encourages the widespread use of content, even as it limits the possibilities of how that information can be organized online. We recall Henry's discussion of the fire hose effect; wandering through the tools and content available online (often organized according to the tune of whichever instructor uploaded it) is like wandering in a used bookstore where every book is free but only the employees know how to find anything. Yes, our Web administrators need to better manage the information online, perhaps using more user-friendly self-organizing tools, but a more fundamental problem hides here as well: the fire hose effect is never going to go away, neither in our program nor in society. How can we help individuals experience agency when they feel overwhelmed with material—and, often enough, unorganized, outdated material? After all, too many choices can quickly seem like no choice at all, which is ultimately an agency issue. Consider the Web technologies introduced during our two weeks of fall 2008 orientation: Share-Point pages for wikis, discussion boards, sharing teaching resources, and maintaining a personal portfolio with syllabi and office hours listed; university-based technologies for checking email, logging into office computers, using shared drives, using library databases, and registering for classes; program-hosted software such as our rubric tool, blogging sites, and wiki sites; and a host of critical Blackboard skills, including basic site organization, creating assignments with dropboxes, managing the grade center, and managing groups, among others. Our plans for upcoming semesters include implementing a simplified teacher dashboard for accessing a number of these pages through a single sign-on location, but findings from our interviews force us to question what else needs simplifying or eliminating. Counterintuitively, it seems that to give too many options may sometimes constitute taking away agency.

Simplicity in our workplace structure also eased contributors' minds about how apparent their contributions would be to others. Many of our online repositories were document libraries and links lists, which had no manual or tacit sorting system for prioritizing the most helpful information—or for bundling similar lesson plans together. The more material contributed, the less important each contribution became. Thus, in an example of the law of diminished utility, each subsequent contribution to our site reduced the clarity and organization of our lists. As we began to account for this irony—that the more people contributed, the more intimidating the site became—faculty responded by becoming more active users of our sites. We accomplished this by realizing that an elegant yet simple design would yield more participation among users and by focusing on a more user-friendly interface. We began with a fairly unstructured approach—a Wild West attitude—but learned it was best to create roles with specific duties.

One of the truisms of modern Web design is that content is king—that readers will come to sites with rich content. From this perspective, the content will become organized as users intuitively learn how to work with one another, synchronizing their work and their websites. But there is another side to the Web, one that involves sites like Facebook, with its $49 billion valuation. These social media sites have prefabricated designs, in which everyone's profile page looks exactly alike and the interface looks identical in every account. Though this identical structure inhibits creativity (Lanier), it also encourages productivity. Facebook is so intuitive that people can focus on sharing: photos, stories, ideas, interests, and activities. Moreover, the simplicity of the site encourages everyone from innovators to late adopters and even laggards to join in (include your own "My mom just created a Facebook account" reference here). The more people join Facebook, the more essential the site becomes. Although we value openness, innovation, and complexity to some extent, we have realized that for blended sites like ours, simplicity is king.

Our suggestion for other WPAs is twofold: organize online materials in the most logical way possible, using the most up-to-date tools available, but also consider training your instructors to develop their own ways of managing this fire hose of data, both as a teaching-sanity measure and as a life skill. We've found that relationships among teachers are often self-organizing, whereas data online aren't—at least not with our current software.

We hope other WPAs will restructure their sites in the way we have realized we need to move: building in ways of organizing the popularity and relevance of contributions based on instructor opinion. We recommend employing some kind of automatic mechanism that allows teachers to vote on the most relevant or helpful online contributions and to have those votes affect which content is most appreciated. Otherwise, teachers will be less inclined to contribute material or sort through what has been uploaded. But on the second issue, we tentatively suggest training instructors to work custom dashboards that use RSS feeds to pull together and filter data in ways that are most meaningful to them. This suggestion is tentative only because of our earlier injunction to focus on student-centered goals; WPAs should be prepared for resistance if training gets too far from discussions of teaching writing.

### 7. Communication Matters.

During this study, we did a number of searches through our listserv records to verify memories of communications, whether uncertainties on our part about what we said when, or when interviewees mentioned a conversation that we wanted to check on. But often, our findings in the records made us seem like better communicators than we expected; quite a few webpages, newsletters, and emails have been sent over the years explaining the rationale for a tool, providing training in a tool's use, or inviting the group to collaborate on modifying the program philosophy statement, rubric language, or project language. So when we hear people critique the program leadership's communication skills, we're faced with an overlapping series of facts: sending someone an email isn't the same as entering into a rich communicative event; people don't always read their emails; memories are contradictory and fallible; sometimes those who seem negative about the program as a whole are actually annoyed at a particular small problem and perfectly understand and subscribe to our datagogical philosophy as a whole.

As much as possible, WPAs need to summon their rhetorical and professional writing skills for all communications—even the briefest emails—to teachers. (We have all experienced that tiny blossom of appreciation at receiving a routine request that feels carefully worded and professionally put together—and therefore, respectful and courteous.) But beyond that, we can make a number of specific suggestions for communicating with instructors:

- Send out written reminders in as many media/formats as possible. We began writing a newsletter for our instructors and another for the university as a whole, distributing them via email. We soon learned that printing out the newsletters in addition to sending them through email garnered more attention, not to mention the push from mentors sharing the information person to person as well. Plus, we discovered that printing the newsletters ensured they were delivered even if the email versions dropped into a spam folder. While deans and other upper administrators rarely responded to our newsletters, we found indirectly that the newsletters were being read outside of the writing program and that they were contributing to our overall reputation as a competent, dedicated community of teachers.

- Structure more face-to-face communication rather than sending only emails or newsletters. We've avoided this in the past because of the unpopularity of pulling so many busy people together at once, and given that the pay of our faculty is predicated on a ten-hour work week per course. But our interviewees' discussions have led us to plan for more required meetings; at the same time, we believe that most of these meetings should be voluntary.

- Use some of these face-to-face meetings for collaborative development of the program's philosophy and curriculum. These experiences in collaborating may lead to stronger buy-in and willingness to contribute in the future. Faculty need to see that administrators are serious about process.

- Reinforce an open-door policy, allowing instructors to take concerns directly to the writing program director, associate director, or mentoring director. Be sure to communicate meeting schedules and agendas in a variety of ways; sending out a mass email with the time, date, and place of the meeting might not be sufficient. Personally invite a small percentage of random instructors and explain why their presence would be welcomed. Populating policy meetings with diverse opinions will result in more voices communicating program progress.

- Regularly reward those who respond to the communications you send. For example, instructor lesson plans sent in response to a mass email were subsequently published in our custom-compiled readers and instructors were thanked as contributors. And when instructors responded to our call for a new handbook by voting for their favorite text and then forming a smaller task force, their preferred handbook was implemented for both ENC 1101 and ENC 1102 courses.

### 8. Dissensus, Diversity, and Underlife Characterize Healthy Communities.

If outsiders were to peer into almost any aspect of our programmatic collaboration, they might notice dissensus, conflict, and confusion. Whether the subject is the curriculum or the policies that drive community decisions, our program's diverse constituencies—writing program staff, adjuncts, graduate teaching assistants, tenured English faculty, university assessment experts, and deans—provide competing advice based on their contrasting values. Though struggling through this dissensus is difficult for any group, our retrospective position has shown that these conflicts are opportunities to improve our program: disagreements force us to clearly articulate our program's most cherished assumptions, and they help us see the weaknesses in any proposed change. In our committee meetings, we've learned as much from critics as from those most agreeable to our program's requirements. Similarly, our instructors have shared with us snippets of a rich underlife, from Lisa's frustrations with the different walled-off "neighborhoods" of teachers, to the satirical rubric emails passed around on the listserv, to Matthew's simple disregard of the requirement to use the online rubric tool, to Audrey's decision to pilot a new writing project in her own way without institutional support or knowledge. But whether these contrasting views are voiced in a meeting or grumbled about in the halls, we have found that the dissenting voices can be the most productive agents of change for programmatic decisions. Dissension and diversity in a meeting lead to compromise that is most acceptable to all sides. Each person is pressed to think through the evidence for his or her own opinion and empathize with contrasting views. Grumbles with real merit continue to grow until they reach a tipping point that topples into needed change; stifling the grumbles would stifle the programmatic growth that comes later.

Many of our decisions are based on open but productive disagreement. For instance, in our FYC Policy Committee (a larger interdepartmental group) and Task Force Committee (a small group of paid staff), dissensus forces every side to provide a rationale and evidence for their opinion. The governing principle is that the most compelling argument in the room has more influence than the professional status of the person arguing it. When we overhauled our curriculum in the summers of 2008 and 2009, our meetings were replete with clashing perspectives. A writing prompt would be written, only to undergo the critical eyes of twenty different instructors, Department of English office staff, and whoever else we could find to take a look. Once after a week of perfecting the language of a new writing project, our office manager, who also holds a master's degree in instructional technology, convinced us to completely rewrite the assignment, showing us how we had failed to address a first-year student audience in terms of organization and diction. Our textbooks, which are self-published, have editors who are chosen in part for their diversity in the ways mentioned throughout this book.

Our suggestion for other programs is that they intentionally structure diverse individuals into decision-making processes—with *diverse* referring both to the categories discussed throughout this study (see Chapter 2 especially) and the diversities specific to a set of FYC instructors. For example, these diversities might include beginning teachers, experienced graduate instructors, adjuncts, and full-time faculty. Those who identify themselves as technological innovators and early adopters will provide a valuable perspective on the potential use of burgeoning technologies, but the early majority, late majority, and laggards will help to broaden perspectives on crowdsourcing. A diverse population will help ensure that each idea proposed goes through a crucible of critical interrogation; it will ensure that each faculty stakeholder group accepts major programmatic decisions as legitimate and well conceived. WPAs need to bring graduate students and adjuncts along, with baby steps, when employing new technologies for grading, communicating with students, or co-constructing a datagogical approach. In the end, we suggest a cautious leaning toward diversity in hiring: don't be afraid to hire even those who outspokenly oppose your point of view as WPAs, but be sure to hire those who are open to change based on dialogue, evidence, and reasoning. It is also important to keep in mind various stakeholder groups, including not just compositionists and rhetoricians but also those pursuing careers in literature, creative writing, and communication studies, depending on the makeup of the instructor population. We suggest that this diversity be planned in at least three areas: committee memberships, paid staff memberships, and online staff. The selection of committee and staff members should also involve some type of democratic or advisory process, perhaps having outgoing members vote on new members, having the entire program faculty vote for representatives, or at the very least providing an opportunity for nomination and volunteerism. Whenever possible all committee meetings should be made public in order to promote a sense of inclusivity.

We have found a variety of online tools (listservs, surveys, forums, wikis, etc.) that can hear the rumblings of a programmatic underlife. Our student surveys (with a typical response rate of 1,000 students each semester) and our teacher surveys (with a response rate of about 40 teachers each semester) have been especially helpful in measuring student needs, interests, and accomplishments. We have always sought ways for instructors and students to "talk back" on our website. We remain committed to employing discussion boards, anonymous comments on blog posts, votes on various kinds of content, and customizable wikis where dissenting voices can be structured and empowered by one another. In addition to technical knowledge, the development of discursive tools requires that administrators consider how students and teachers prioritize privacy and ethos online. This has been a recurring need for our program as teachers provide feedback about what they are comfortable uploading within a private or public site online. In past years, our teachers have requested that some online collaboration between faculty be blocked from student viewing. From their perspective, open discussions about pedagogy could undermine their authority in the classroom.

We point to Paulo's leadership on the rubric subcommittee as evidence of the ideal relationship of an instructor to the wider program, and of one way that gaps between ideologies can be smoothed over through individual and collective engagement: individual frustration leads to banding together a group of like-minded individuals, who then are empowered to create change and thus become increasingly willing to accept the changes that others have made through the same process of engagement.

But we also recognize that for some, initial resistance is inevitable, and therefore less something for WPAs to fear than to be prepared for. We are comforted by understanding that the resistance we face is similar to the resistance Sally Barr Ebest faced when training TAs to teach at her institution (over the course of five years, 80 percent of men and 20 percent of women initially resisted her pedagogy).

### 9. Process Is Inevitable, but Frustrations Will Continue.

With its emphasis on process, a datagological model may engender some confusion and frustration, especially for those teachers who want the curriculum done once and for all. Related to Henry's concerns, we recall how the process of changing our program, online and offline, can be seen as simultaneously responsive and bewildering. For example, when an FYC staff member suggested during the fall 2008 orientation that the group of seventy-plus instructors continue talking about the language on our rubric using yet another peer-production tool, one graduate instructor stood up and cried out "No!" She felt that the conversation had no limits and would never be resolved with such an open-ended impromptu format. Later in the semester, however, when Paulo led a rubric committee that produced a detailed report with suggestions and feedback, the results were invaluable. Paulo's report involved a much more structured system for introducing complaints, concerns, and ideas. Now, years later, revisions still circulate through various committees.

In 2002 no one had heard of Facebook, yet now some instructors use it as a type of virtual space for office hours. In 2000 very few people were blogging, and now we have articles about the "death of blogging." Wikis were the frontier five years ago, and now they are well-worn experiences for many and perhaps losing ground to tools like Google Docs. Twitter is now being discussed as a pedagogical tool in some conferences and journals. We have changed our main website for usability reasons, abandoned wikis because of security issues, and reconsidered many times the efficacy of blogging for a curriculum focused on academic writing. Technologies should not be abandoned because they become unfashionable but rather because they no longer meet the needs of students and teachers.

*10. The Role of the Writing Program Administrator Is Shifting from the Central Authority to the Community Manager.*
The presence of peer-production tools means that most communities—with or without the permission of administrators—will exist in both online and face-to-face settings. As individuals, teachers will also influence and be influenced by programs, departments, colleges, universities, and groundswell movements (such as online teacher evaluation sites) with or without their consent. Therefore,

the savvy individual and the socially conscious administrator will examine the ways that individual and communal agency operate and how every tool, including but not limited to peer-production technologies, can be used to create a more transparent, accountable, and democratic interplay between teacher, student, and administrator.

Innovator, master teacher, autocrat, dictator, pit boss—the writing program administrator can play any number of roles, reflecting differences in program design, university governance, and vision. While depictions of writing programs and WPAs vary, the most common model, as Jeanne Gunner observes in "Decentering the WPA," is the "WPA-centric model"—a model in which information flows from the one to the many, in which the WPA is the sole tenured faculty member, the house authority on all things composition; in which graduate teaching assistants and adjuncts are characterized as lesser-qualified technicians. This model of writing program administration may have seemed cutting edge back in the 1980s when Olson and Moxley's research found that department chairs preferred weak, nontenured WPAs who lacked disciplinary expertise. But since the early 1990s, power has flowed into the position of WPA, as universities have recognized the need to hire tenured faculty who hold doctorates in composition and rhetoric to administer writing programs. Over the past two decades, it has become commonplace for universities to value strong writing program administrators, scholars, and researchers who can lead campuswide writing efforts, who ground their visions in research and scholarship and experience.

Now, thanks to peer-production and social media tools, the work of WPAs is once again being reconceived. Only this time, rather than reflecting the legitimization of composition studies as an academic field, the change most fully impacts teachers and the ways WPAs work with them. While in the past it was nearly impossible, especially in large writing programs, for WPAs to know what was going on in the classrooms of their teachers, now, thanks to social media and peer-production tools, WPAs can easily peer into individual classrooms. From a power perspective, teachers could be demoted to technicians who teach the lessons of the WPA: WPAs can gather information about the length of time teachers spend grading papers and the diversity and preciseness of their feedback. They can measure instructor grading in terms of standard deviations from the norm. In practically real time, they can gather student evaluations, determine whether instructors are holding office hours or canceling classes, and even control the scheduling of assignments. Given that agency resides in how people use tools, this panoptican gaze can be manipulated to facilitate either a culture of power or a culture of learning (Moxley, "Datagogies"). From our perspective, WPAs should be vigilant in their efforts to facilitate a "community of learning" (Blake) and protect faculty from a more myopic, command-and-control leadership style.

## CONCLUSION

Higher education is ripe for change. Students are graduating from high schools, yet their test scores suggest they lack the writing and critical thinking skills necessary to succeed in college. Students face skyrocketing education costs at the same time that state support for education is dwindling, which forces them to work more out of school and spend less time on their course work. And those of us who teach tell a common story, that students aren't coming to class, with attendance sometimes dropping dramatically by the end of the semester. Even after completing several years of course work, college students' test scores nationwide do not indicate improvement as writers or critical thinkers. As sociologists Richard Arum and Josipa Roksa report in *Academically Adrift: Limited Learning on College Campuses*, "45 percent of students" do not improve their "critical thinking, complex reasoning, and writing skills" for a variety of reasons, such as studying in groups, participating in social activities, or attending a college that values research over teaching (121–22). The report calls into question the value students receive from a college education, noting that many courses are not sufficiently challenging. In response to these current challenges in higher education, Gerald Graff has argued that courseocentrism undermines the rigor of our programs and the training of our faculty ("Why Assessment?"). He has chided faculty for rejecting any and all claims at standardization and argues that courseocentrism is one of the impediments to student learning that higher education needs to change.

Our research provides evidence for how to implement standardization without strangling academic freedom. Broadly speaking, our research challenges two dominant assumptions of the US educational system: (1) standardization of a curriculum is invariably anti-democratic and pernicious, and (2) the barrier between the closed classroom door and public discourse is sacrosanct—that is, composition curricula should primarily be authored by tenured professors or imported from a professional organization such as NCTE, as opposed to being debated, revised, and coauthored by many teachers in a program, including teachers who are in training as graduate students or adjuncts.

We have found that composition teachers and writing program administrators can use peer-production tools to collaborate with one another on a shared pedagogy. We think there are several benefits to this, the primary one being that teachers are in the best position to define the curriculum; often WPAs do not teach first-year composition courses. Thus, teachers may have a better sense of their students because they know their preferred learning styles. And, by using social media and peer-production tools, large groups of teachers can work with one another and with WPAs for the first time to share resources, assessment information, and expertise. This more holistic approach to curriculum development—and, in time, of integrating assessment into the curriculum development process—creates the opportunity for a new sort of pedagogy, a datagogy, that can be used across disciplines. Its hallmarks are transparency, sharing, clarity, and focus. In this approach, agency does not need to be a zero-sum game, a tug of war between instructors and administrators. New opportunities for creativity such as custom textbooks compiled by instructors, mentoring, and online collaboration require some conformity but yield otherwise out-of-reach opportunities. Peer production giveth and it taketh away.

In the years ahead, particularly as universities continue to hire adjuncts and graduate students rather than tenured professors, we think universities have a lot to gain by creating datagogies—interactive pedagogical sites that empower teachers to share resources and to collaborate on a shared pedagogy around clearly defined outcomes, sites that provide rich assessment data that teachers can use to recognize needed curricular revisions.

Yet change is never easy.

In Jay David Bolter's *Writing Space*, he refers to Victor Hugo's *Notre-Dame de Paris, 1482,* in which a priest reflects on ways the printed book will replace the authority of the church. The priest remarks, "Ceci tuera cela": This book will destroy that building. The priest meant not only that printing and literacy would undermine the authority of the church but also that "human thought . . . would change its mode of expression, that the principal idea of each generation would no longer write itself with the same material and in the same way, that the book of stone, so solid and durable, would give place to the book made of paper, yet more solid and durable" (199). Bolter uses this story to introduce his prescient analysis of how hypertext could remediate the traditional linear print book. We wonder if this same story is reflective of how peer-production technologies and social media could transform education. Regardless of how this story ends, we are convinced that agency will play a lead role, that agency will be a character who undergoes a powerful character development, and that it is up to us to determine whether that development is beneficial.

**WORKS CITED**

**INDEX**

## WORKS CITED

Althusser, Louis. *Lenin and Philosophy and Other Essays.* Trans. Ben Brewster. New York: Monthly Review, 1971. Print.

Anderson, Chris. "People Power." *Wired.* Condé Nast Digital, July 2006. Web. 13 May 2010.

Arum, Richard, and Josipa Roksa. *Academically Adrift: Limited Learning on College Campuses.* Chicago: U of Chicago P, 2011. Print.

Bakhtin, M. M. "Discourse in the Novel." *The Dialogic Imagination: Four Essays.* Trans. Caryl Emerson and Michael Holquist. Ed. Michael Holquist. Austin: U of Texas P, 1981. 259–422. Print.

Behar, Ruth. "Ethnography in a Time of Blurred Genres." *Anthropology and Humanism* 32.2 (2007): 145–55. Print.

Benkler, Yochai. *The Wealth of Networks: How Social Production Transforms Markets and Freedom.* New Haven, CT: Yale UP, 2006. Print.

Benkler, Yochai, and Helen Nissenbaum. "Commons-Based Peer Production and Virtue." *Journal of Political Philosophy* 14.4 (2006): 394–419. Print.

Blake, Elizabeth S. "Talking about Research: Are We Playing Someone Else's Game?" *The Politics and Processes of Scholarship.* Ed. Joseph M. Moxley and Lagretta T. Lenker. Westport, CT: Greenwood, 1995. 27–39. Print.

Blythe, Stuart. "Agencies, Ecologies, and the Mundane Artifacts in Our Midst." *Labor, Writing Technologies, and the Shaping of Composition in the Academy.* Ed. Pamela Takayoshi and Patricia Sullivan. Cresskill, NJ: Hampton, 2006. 167–86. Print.

Bolter, Jay David. *Writing Space: The Computer, Hypertext, and the History of Writing.* Hillsdale, NJ: Erlbaum, 1991. Print.

boyd, danah m., and Nicole B. Ellison. "Social Network Sites: Definition, History, and Scholarship." *Journal of Computer-Mediated Communication* 13.1 (2007): n. pag. Web. 13 May 2010.

Boyer, Ernest L. *Scholarship Reconsidered: Priorities of the Professoriate.* Princeton, NJ: Carnegie Foundation for the Advancement of Teaching, 1990. Print.

Boyle, Peg, and Bob Boice. "Systematic Mentoring for New Faculty Teachers and Graduate Teaching Assistants." *Innovative Higher Education* 22.3 (1998): 157–79. Print.

Breland, Hunter M. *The Direct Assessment of Writing Skill: A Measurement Review.* New York: College Entrance Examination Board, 1983. Print.

Brooke, Robert. "Underlife and Writing Instruction." *College Composition and Communication* 38.2 (1987): 141–53. *JSTOR.* Web. 13 May 2010.

Brown, John Seely, and Paul Duguid. *The Social Life of Information.* Boston: Harvard Business School P, 2000. Print.

Campbell, Clark D. "Best Practices for Student–Faculty Mentoring Programs." *The Blackwell Handbook of Mentoring: A Multiple Perspectives Approach.* Ed. Tammy D. Allen and Lillian T. Eby. Malden, MA: Wiley-Blackwell, 2010. 325–43. Print.

Carroll, Lee Ann. *Rehearsing New Roles: How College Students Develop as Writers.* Carbondale: Southern Illinois UP, 2002. Print.

Charney, Davida. "The Validity of Using Holistic Scoring to Evaluate Writing: A Critical Overview." *Research in the Teaching of English* 18.1 (1984): 65–81. Print.

Chiseri-Strater, Elizabeth. *Academic Literacies: The Public and Private Discourse of University Students.* Portsmouth, NH: Boynton/Cook, 1991. Print.

Connors, Robert J., and Andrea A. Lunsford. "Teachers' Rhetorical Comments on Student Papers." *College Composition and Communication* 44.2 (1993): 200–23. Print.

Cummings, Robert E., and Matt Barton, eds. *Wiki Writing: Collaborative Learning in the College Classroom.* Ann Arbor: U of Michigan P, 2008. Print.

Diederich, Paul B. *Measuring Growth in English.* Urbana, IL: NCTE, 1974. Print.

Durst, Russel K. *Collision Course: Conflict, Negotiation, and Learning in College Composition.* Urbana, IL: NCTE, 1999. Print.

Ebest, Sally Barr. *Changing the Way We Teach: Writing and Resistance in the Training of Teaching Assistants.* Carbondale: Southern Illinois UP, 2005. Print.

Elbow, Peter. "Do We Need a Single Standard of Value for Institutional Assessment? An Essay Response to Asao Inoue's 'Community-Based Assessment Pedagogy.'" *Assessing Writing* 11.2 (2006): 81–99. Print.

———. *Embracing Contraries: Explorations in Learning and Teaching.* New York: Oxford UP, 1986. Print.

———. "Ranking, Evaluating, and Liking: Sorting Out Three Forms of Judgment." *College English* 55.2 (1993): 187–206. Print.

Ellis, Carolyn, and Arthur P. Bochner, eds. *Composing Ethnography: Alternative Forms of Qualitative Writing.* Walnut Creek, CA: AltaMira, 1996. Print.

Foster, David. *Writing with Authority: Students' Roles as Writers in Cross-National Perspective.* Carbondale: Southern Illinois UP, 2006. Print.

Gillmor, Dan. *We the Media: Grassroots Journalism by the People, for the People.* Sebastopol, CA: O'Reilly, 2004. Print.

Graff, Gerald. "It's Time to End 'Courseocentrism.'" *Inside Higher Ed.* Inside Higher Ed, 13 Jan. 2009. Web. 3 Jan. 2011.

———. "Why Assessment?" *Pedagogy* 10.1 (2010): 153–65. Print.

Gunner, Jeanne. "Collaborative Administration." *The Writing Program Administrator's Resource: A Guide to Reflective Institutional Practice.* Ed. Stuart C. Brown, Theresa Enos, and Catherine Chaput. Mahwah, NJ: Erlbaum, 2002. 253–62. Print.

———. "Decentering the WPA." *WPA* 18.1-2 (1994): 8–15. *Council of Writing Program Administrators.* Web. 3 Jan. 2011.

Habermas, Jürgen. *The Structural Transformation of the Public Sphere: An Inquiry into a Category of Bourgeois Society.* Trans. Thomas Burger. Cambridge, MA: MIT P, 1991. Print.

Holbrook, Sue Ellen. "Women's Work: The Feminizing of Composition." *Rhetoric Review* 9.2 (1991): 201–29. Print.

Jacobi, Maryann. "Mentoring and Undergraduate Academic Success: A Literature Review." *Review of Educational Research* 61.4 (1991): 505–32. Print.

Jaschik, Scott. "What Direction for Rhet-Comp?" *Inside Higher Ed.* Inside Higher Ed, 30 Dec. 2009. Web. 13 May 2010.

Jenkins, Henry. *Convergence Culture: Where Old and New Media Collide.* New York: New York UP, 2006. Print.

Kemp, Fred. "Computers, Innovation, and Resistance in First-Year Composition Programs." *Discord and Direction: The Postmodern Writing Program Administrator.* Ed. Sharon James McGee and Carolyn Handa. Logan: Utah State UP, 2005. 105–22. Print.

Kutz, Eleanor, and Hephzibah Roskelly. *An Unquiet Pedagogy: Transforming Practice in the English Classroom.* Portsmouth, NH: Boynton/Cook, 1991. Print.

Lamott, Anne. *Bird by Bird: Some Instructions on Writing and Life.* New York: Anchor, 1995. Print.

Lanier, Jaron. *You Are Not a Gadget: A Manifesto.* New York: Knopf, 2010. Print.

Lewis, Lyndsey. "Florida Universities Brace for Budget Cuts." *Chronicle of Higher Education.* Chronicle of Higher Education, 27 July 2007. Web. 13 May 2010.

Li, Charlene, and Josh Bernoff. *Groundswell: Winning in a World Transformed by Social Technologies.* Boston: Harvard Business School P, 2008. Print.

Lincoln, Yvonna S., and Egon G. Guba. *Naturalistic Inquiry.* Newbury Park, CA: Sage, 1985. Print.

Malouff, John. "Bias in Grading." *College Teaching* 56.3 (2008): 191–92. Print.

Matus, Ron. "University of South Florida St. Petersburg Placed on Accreditation Probation." *St. Petersburg Times.* St. Petersburg Times, 28 June 2008. Web. 13 May 2010.

McGuire, Gail M., and Jo Reger. "Feminist Co-Mentoring: A Model for Academic Professional Development." *NWSA Journal* 15.1 (2003): 54–72. Print.

Mitchell, Candace. *Writing and Power: A Critical Introduction to Composition Studies.* Boulder, CO: Paradigm, 2004. Print.

Moxley, Joseph M. "Datagogies, Writing Spaces, and the Age of Peer Production." *Computers and Composition* 25.2 (2008): 182–202. Print.

———. "Responding to Student Writing: Goals, Methods, Alternatives." *Freshman English News* 17.2 (1989): 3–4; 9–11. Print.

———. "Teachers' Goals and Methods of Responding to Student Writing." *Composition Studies: English Freshman News* 20.1 (1992): 17–33. Print.

Mueller, Derek. "Call: *CCCarnival.*" *Earth Wide Moth.* 14 July 2008. Web. 13 May 2010.

Nye, Joseph S. *The Powers to Lead.* Oxford: Oxford UP, 2008. Print.

Olson, Gary A., and Joseph M. Moxley. "Directing Freshman Composition: The Limits of Authority." *College Composition and Communication* 40.1 (1989): 51–60. Print.

Porter, James E., Patricia Sullivan, Stuart Blythe, Jeffrey T. Grabill, and Libby Miles. "Institutional Critique: A Rhetorical Methodology for Change." *College Composition and Communication* 51.4 (2000): 610–42. Print.

Raban, Daphne R., and Eyal Rabin. "Statistical Inference from Power Law Distributed Web-Based Social Interactions." *Internet Research* 19.3 (2009): 266–78. Print.

Rezaei, Ali Reza, and Michael Lovorn. "Reliability and Validity of Rubrics for Assessment through Writing." *Assessing Writing* 15.1 (2010): 18–39. Print.

Rheingold, Howard. *Smart Mobs: The Next Social Revolution*. Cambridge, MA: Perseus, 2002. Print.

Rogers, Everett M. *Diffusion of Innovations*. 1962. 4th ed. New York: Free Press, 1995. Print.

Scannell, Dale P., and Jon C. Marshall. "The Effect of Selected Composition Errors on Grades Assigned to Essay Examinations." *American Educational Research Journal* 3.2 (1966): 125–30. Print.

Shaughnessy, Mina P. *Errors and Expectations: A Guide for the Teacher of Basic Writing*. New York: Oxford UP, 1977. Print.

Shirky, Clay. *Here Comes Everybody: The Power of Organizing without Organizations*. New York: Penguin, 2008. Print.

Shor, Ira, and Paulo Freire. *A Pedagogy for Liberation: Dialogues on Transforming Education*. South Hadley, MA: Bergin and Garvey, 1987. Print.

Siemens, George. *Knowing Knowledge*. 2006. *elearnspace*. Web. 14 May 2010.

Sohn, Katherine Kelleher. *Whistlin' and Crowin' Women of Appalachia: Literacy Practices since College*. Carbondale: Southern Illinois UP, 2006. Print.

Sommers, Nancy. "Responding to Student Writing." *College Composition and Communication* 33.2 (1982): 148–56. *JSTOR*. Web. 8 Feb. 2008.

Starch, Daniel, and Edward C. Elliott. "Reliability of the Grading of High-School Work in English." *School Review* 20.7 (1912): 442–57. Print.

"Statistics." *Facebook*. Facebook, n.d. Web. 14 May 2010.

Stern, Lesa A., and Amanda Solomon. "Effective Faculty Feedback: The Road Less Traveled." *Assessing Writing* 11.1 (2006): 22–41. Print.

Sullivan, Patricia, and James E. Porter. *Opening Spaces: Writing Technologies and Critical Research Practices*. Westport, CT: Ablex, 1997. Print.

Surowiecki, James. *The Wisdom of Crowds*. New York: Anchor, 2004. Print.

Tapscott, Don, and Anthony D. Williams. *Wikinomics: How Mass Collaboration Changes Everything*. New York: Portfolio, 2006. Print.

Taylor, Mark C. "End the University as We Know It." *New York Times*. New York Times, 26 Apr. 2009. Web. 13 May 2010.

Tinberg, Howard B. *Border Talk: Writing and Knowing in the Two-Year College*. Urbana, IL: NCTE, 1997. Print.

Trimbur, John. "Agency and the Death of the Author: A Partial Defense of Modernism." *JAC* 20.2 (2000): 283–98. Print.

Tuell, Cynthia. "Composition Teaching as 'Women's Work': Daughters, Handmaids, Whores, and Mothers." *Writing Ourselves into the Story: Unheard Voices from Composition Studies.* Ed. Sheryl I. Fontaine and Susan Hunter. Carbondale: Southern Illinois UP, 1993. 123–39. Print.

Wallace, Ray, and Susan Lewis Wallace. "Growing Our Own: Writing Centers as Historically Fertile Fields for Professional Development." *The Writing Center Director's Sourcebook.* Ed. Christina Murphy and Byron L. Stay. Mahwah, NJ: Erlbaum, 2006. 45–52. Print.

Weinberger, David. *Everything is Miscellaneous: The Power of the New Digital Disorder.* New York: Times Books, 2007. Print.

Wilson, Chris. "The Wisdom of the Chaperones." *Slate.* Slate Group, Washington Post, 22 Feb. 2008. Web. 3 Aug. 2011.

Winston, Morton. "Prospects for a Revaluation of Academic Values." *The Politics and Processes of Scholarship.* Ed. Joseph M. Moxley and Lagretta T. Lenker. Westport, CT: Greenwood, 1995. 53–66. Print.

Yancey, Kathleen Blake. "Looking Back as We Look Forward: Historicizing Writing Assessment." *College Composition and Communication* 50.3 (1999): 483–503. Print.

———. "(Still) Historicizing Assessment: Postings on Looking Back as We Look Forward." University of South Florida, Tampa. 5 Feb. 2010. Address.

# INDEX

## AUTHORS

**Quentin D. Vieregge,** http://quentinvieregge .com, is an assistant professor of English at the University of Wisconsin–Barron County. Vieregge has published on cult branding in popular culture and has a chapter, which is accepted and under review, on exigency in student writing in the Writing Spaces series. He currently serves as managing editor for Writing Commons, http://writingcommons .org, an open education resource, and as director of writing at UW–BC's The Learning Center.

**Kyle D. Stedman** is an assistant professor of English at Rockford College. He is interested in the rhetoric of sound and music, intellectual property, multimodal composition pedagogy, and fan studies. His work has appeared in *Computers and Composition, Currents in Electronic Literacy,* and the Writing Spaces series of textbooks, for which he serves as an assistant editor.

A visiting instructor and MA advisor at the University of South Florida, **Taylor Joy Mitchell** recently completed her dissertation, which analyzes the literature published in *Playboy* magazine during the Cold War. At USF, she teaches Contemporary and Modern Literature, Introduction to Literature, Expository Writing, and Cultural Studies and the Popular Arts. She has published in the fields of literature and popular culture but continues to focus her research and energy on pedagogical matters.

A professor of English and director of first-year composition at the University of South Florida, **Joseph M. Moxley,** http://joemoxley.org, is currently working on http://writingcommons .org, a free, open education resource, and http:// myreviewers.usf.edu/, a Web-based resource that enables teachers and students to use rubrics and commenting tools to review and grade student writing. Moxley has published on a variety of topics, including qualitative research methodologies, digital libraries, learning communities, assessment, and scholarly publishing. Moxley's *College Writing Online* received the 2003 *Computers and Composition* Distinguished Book Award.

## OTHER BOOKS IN THE CCCC STUDIES IN WRITING & RHETORIC SERIES

This book was typeset in Garamond and Frutiger by Barbara Frazier.
Typefaces used on the cover include Adobe Garamond and Formata.
The book was printed on 55-lb. Natural Offset paper
by Victor Graphics, Inc.